The Intuitive Gardener

The Man Behind the
Ananda Meditation Retreat Garden

The Intuitive Gardener

The Man Behind the
Ananda Meditation Retreat Garden

By **Charles M. Evans**

As told to Biraj Palmer

The Intuitive Gardener: The Man Behind the
Ananda Meditation Retreat Garden

By Charles Evans as told to Biraj Palmer

Blue Bone Books
300 Jims Road
Ben Lomond, CA 95005

ISBN #: 978-1-948675-19-2
Library of Congress: 2025900570

Book Design by Anaya Gamow and Mobeen Fazal
Photos by Barbara Bingham and Kent Williams

Blue Bone Books
Santa Cruz, CA

IN GRATITUDE

Special thanks to the following people without whose help and inspiration this book would not have come into fruition:

Durga Smallen, Anandi Cornell, Devi Novak, Jyotish Novak,
Barbara Bingham, Kent Williams, Anaya Gamow, Lakshmi Selbie,
Swami Kriyananda, Asha Nayaswami, Shanti Rubenstone, Mobeen Fazal,
Narayani Anaya, Mahavir Hernandez, David James, Robin Lysne,
Elvin Raja, Dana Andersen, and most especially
my beloved wife Lahari Palmer.

DEDICATION

This book is dedicated:
to Ruth, my friend through the ages,
to Rick, my brother and life-long friend, and
to Ananda, special to me for nurturing my soul.

Table of Contents

2000s

Forward

The Intuitive Gardener presents the life of a remarkable man, Charles Evans, who has been blessed with two great gifts: deep intuitive perception, and the courage to follow his intuition. His whole life is a remarkable example of how a higher plan for inner growth exists for each of us, if we are open to the unexpected.

I first met Charles in 1992, as he described in one of the chapters of the book. At our first meeting, I could tell that he operated on a different wavelength than most people—it seemed that he approached everything from an inner attunement or oneness with it, rather than just relating to the outer form.

Over the years when we spoke together, I could feel that he didn't really communicate through words, but through a subtler perception. For this reason, it was always a great joy to converse with him, because one could feel that the real exchange took place on a silent, heart level filled with love.

The Intuitive Gardener is told in Charles' own words, recorded by his friend, Biraj Palmer, in interviews over several years. I'm immensely grateful to Biraj for his devoted work in compiling and transcribing these interviews. They give us not only the unusual story of Charles' life, but also a guide for how we, too, can live if we are open to new paths that open before us.

Equally important in this book is the fact that Charles is a gifted gardener. This skill runs through his whole life story. Since 2001 he dedicated himself to creating, among other sites, the extraordinary gardens at Ananda Meditation Retreat near Nevada City, California. When one walks through these beautiful gardens, you can sense that a different kind of "planning" created this fluid array of flowers, trees, shrines, fountains, bird feeders, and ponds—hence the title of the book: *The Intuitive Gardener.*

It is an honor to know the man whose life it presents. As I read his story, I became aware that what at first seemed like a random series of events in his life were all part of a greater plan for the expansion of his consciousness. The beautiful natural gardens that he has created all over the world are only reflections of the garden of his soul. In this inner haven he dwells with increasing awareness of his oneness with all of life and with God.

Nayaswami Devi Novak
Co-Spiritual Director of Ananda Sangha Worldwide
Ananda Village, CA

Introduction

The idea for this book started back in the summer of 1996, when Charles Evans and I spent a long twilight evening dangling our legs over the edge of the stage overlooking Lotus Lake at Ananda's Expanding Light Retreat. Charles regaled me with story after story of his life growing up. I will never forget the joyful mirth of the tales that I heard that memorable evening, surrounded by the chirping of a thousand singing crickets, and a billion twinkling stars. As the years went by, Charles and I would manage to connect for long chats a couple times each year, whether we lived close by each other or not. His stories always left me in fits of laughter. And many of them blew my mind. I'd never met anyone who lived his life like this. To say Charles is eccentric is to put it mildly. But his life has a charm, a passion, a heart wide open to what life gives him. He engages aspects of life most of us hardly notice. And ... he listens.

It's that aspect of Charles' story that I kept being struck by. He doesn't only listen to people—we all try to do that. But he listens to what the Universe is saying to him. And that's something few of us are as good at as we could be. And it turns out—who knew? —the Universe has a sense of humor!

Charles enjoys a minor fame among the visitors to Ananda Village near Nevada City, California because of what he has accomplished over the years on a dry, dusty hilltop at Ananda's Meditation Retreat. The place has been used by meditators for quiet seclusion since Swami Kriyananda established it in the late 1960's. But for decades, though graced with a deep calm and quietness, the spot was choked with tall, scraggly manzanita bushes—

thousands of them all packed together. It was easy to get lost amidst them, especially at night or after a snowfall. The spooky, other worldliness of the place wasn't helped by the three mile "dirt" road that one had to traverse in order to find the Meditation Retreat. To call the road "dirt" is being kind, since in reality for many years it was one of the rockiest roads you'd ever negotiated, with big chucks of rock banging up under your vehicle, and even bigger potholes threatening to swallow whole any inattentive driver's car during the lengthy bad seasons—which could be even worse in summer than in winter!

But the garden ... Nothing of it existed at all until 1994. Even then, it remained quite modest as late as 2004. But for the past two decades, Charles has wielded his magic—or rather Someone's magic—to create what we see today. And how that happened, is a story worth telling.

Anyway, in the summer of 2016, I arrived, with recorder in hand, to Charles' simple wooden home down past the crest of the Meditation Retreat's hilltop. Having called ahead to warn him of my invasion, Charles started right off by asking, "Now, what is it you're looking for?"

"I hope that when we're done, that we will have collected a lot of the stories that you, Charles, have told people over the years, so that not just one or 25 or 100 people could have heard them, but thousands of people will have the chance to experience them. About the garden, of course, but also, if you'd be willing, I bet people would appreciate a bit of the biographical stuff that came before the garden—that got you to this point. I'd like to find out what it was like when you spent time at the Findhorn training place. I'd like to know what it was like when you were in New York City doing the art gallery, or at the hairdressers' place. Over the years that we've known each other, you've told me things like, 'I was the Qualified Building Engineer, though I wasn't really qualified for it,' a position which you also identified as 'the Super, the fix-it guy, but all I really did was I listened to the place.' "

"Kind of like what you do at the Meditation Retreat, but with the *plants*! We want to know what the guy went through that ended up doing this amazing garden!"

"How I got here?"

"Yes. I don't know that there's anything to leave out! Anything that's a fun story that helped make you the man you've become. I think people would love to hear it."

"You want my life story?"

"Only to create a context. It's first and foremost a story about how your garden came to be. I'm not thinking it'll be a complete biography, but maybe something more like this: here is the previous life, and here's what he did with it. I think it will end up with a lot less stories of the early days than there will be of the last 20 years" (now 30!), "but I bet the earlier ones will have a place, too ... More than merely a story about you, Charles, I see this as a story about how the Divine has made use of a soul who was willing to listen."

"And that's the reason I agreed to do it! That's my whole mission with the garden tours and everything I do here. If I can do it, you can do it, too! It's all about tuning in."

And so, it began ...

Biraj Wayne Palmer
Palo Alto, CA
September 12, 2024

1940s

YOUTH

I was born in August of 1939. When I was young, I was very shy, very quiet, very withdrawn. I remember one day thinking the startling revelation that, "No one knows how I feel unless I tell them." But otherwise, I don't remember much about my time as a child.

I do remember that I had polio when I was 9 or 10 years old. I was racing to catch the school bus, and on the way I fell. That's when I knew something was wrong. I kept telling mom that I'd been falling, but she thought it was just growing pains. On the way to the bus, suddenly I collapsed. The next thing I knew Mom had swooped me in her arms, threw me in the car, took me to the doctor—polio was big then—and barged ahead of everybody. Mothers will do that, my mother especially. He had her sit down, and he says, "Your son has had polio, but he's through with it. It's been a very mild case. And these are just the after-effects." I'd had it and hadn't even known I'd had it. But it affected me. It wiped out muscles in my legs. It wiped out muscles in my diaphragm. I ended up having to take tap dancing lessons to strengthen my bad leg. It's affecting me even more now as I grow older, as happens with a number of polio survivors. I get strange cramps. Kriya can be challenging because of polio's effect on the diaphragm.

When I was a child of about 9, our refrigerator broke. I was born in 1939, so this happened right after WWII, and money was still tight. The repairman came out to try to fix it, but left saying, "This thing can't be fixed. You have to get a new one." I went in, took the front off, and stared at the motor for a long while. Then my mother said my little hands did something and suddenly the thing worked, and it ran without any trouble at all for another 10 years. I just have some kind of relationship with machinery. It responds to me. I just knew how to do things. But I thought everybody was like that.

It's a talent. It runs in my family. It's the Italian side. They've always been a little bit psychic. Now, we were Catholic, so it was suppressed. But Italians are speaking to the other side all the time. One of the lines I loved in *The Secret of Findhorn* book was, "Dorothy was raised Catholic, but like so many mystics in our times she was surrounded by a church that was not supportive of you actually talking to God—let alone listening to Him."

The people in my family just knew things. My grandfather had died early on. So, I was left with a grandmother who had 4 daughters. And they just *knew*.

Mom was full-blooded Italian. All my aunts were Italian, too, but somehow, they had chutzpah.[1] We were a big, loud, raucous Italian family. They used to embarrass me no end, hanging out of car windows, things like that. I would be scrunched down below the window, not wanting to be seen with them. I always felt like a square peg in a round hole.

My grandfather must have come to the States during the 19aughts, and sent for my grandmother later on, because my mother was born in 1913. Grandma Ciola, the matriarch of the family, came over from Italy. Grandma arrived at Ellis Island with no English, nobody to meet her, and was able to get to Missouri all on her own. My grandfather was mining in Missouri. My mother was born there. Shortly afterwards, my grandmother moved the family out of there, because my grandfather was gambling and drinking all the time with the other miners. Grandma wanted to give him a better environment.

So, they moved to Florida. There was a small Italian community in Fort Pierce, Florida, so that's where they headed. They saved up some money and bought an orange grove. It was 60 miles from West Palm Beach where my own mother grew up. My grandparents still weren't married, because there hadn't been a Catholic priest anywhere nearby.

When my mother's younger sister Pauline was born, and they took her to be baptized, the priest wouldn't baptize her because her parents weren't married. So, my grandparents drove across the state to Tampa to get married, where the priest wouldn't know that they already had two kids. That way, as an older couple they finally got married, so they could get the newest kid baptized.

My grandfather, a drinker, died when my mother was 13. My grandmother, from that point on, ran the orange grove all by herself, dug all the ditches, everything. My grandma was a strong lady. I loved my grandma. As kids, we used to follow her all around the grove. She was terrific.

My own parents married in the late 1930's, and I was born in 1939. My mom Emma and my father Charles ran a diner called Charlie's Corner. He had been a butcher early in life, but then in the early 1940's they opened the restaurant in West Palm Beach--stools at a counter, and little booths. My brother and I used to wait tables. When you're the kids of a restaurant owner, you pitch in.

Very soon, though, after they bought the diner, World War II broke out, and my father got called up into the Navy. He went in as a cook but never got out of the States. While he was away doing his patriotic duty, my mother was running the business, to the point that she was having a nervous breakdown. But the family knew some important politician—maybe even the governor. They pulled strings to get my father discharged and sent home, so that Mom wouldn't completely freak out trying to keep the business going alone.

Mom was a tough lady, but there was a delicate part of her. She was over-nervous. She went to the doctor once during all of this. And he told her, "You're to go home, and open your kitchen cabinet, and empty everything out into the middle of the floor—your pots and pans, everything. And then throw ‘em back in, but not in order." She was being too precise, too micromanaging everything. So she did that, and it did seem to help. She seemed fine after that.

My parents ran the diner all the time that my brother and I were young, all the way through until high school. Then we lost it. Right across the street from the diner, AT&T had its big main facility. Their workers were the mainstay of my father's business. But then all those workers went on a several-month strike against AT&T, and my parents lost all their customers.

The business was probably going down-hill before that. My father had already gotten back into his alcoholism. So, he lost that business. Since he had been in the Navy, we were able to send him to the VA hospital, and they re-did him. Dried him out, fixed his teeth, fixed his varicose veins. He came back for a while and went back to being a meat butcher. But he got into alcohol again, and to make it worse he was a sloppy drunk. I especially remember being embarrassed that his feet stank. Finally, Mom kicked him out for good. Actually, I didn't have much to do with my father.

Just before she kicked him out, all of us had to go out and get jobs. There was no money.

So, my brother and I got paper routes. I wasn't 16 yet. Mom got a job at Burdine's, a fancy department store. It was like Macy's or Bloomingdale's out here in California. She was beautiful, so worked in cosmetics. When I turned 16, I got a job at Burdine's, too.

I remember as a child—must have been in upper grade school— I was reading books about the South Sea islands, and detective books. You've got to remember that I lived in Florida, where nothing ever happened. It was kind of like how Californians think of the Midwest. I remember thinking, "You know, nothing exciting ever happens here. People in these books always have a wonderful time, yet here I've got this boring life. I'm going to need more excitement."

I started to be a sneaky rebel. My poor brother, I used to get my little brother into so much trouble. He got blamed for everything. He did have a wild side. He was always more rajasic, more of a Leo. My parents were forced to pull him out of Catholic school, because he and a nun were always fighting. I got away with things because I was a little more sattwic[2], and I must have looked innocent. He always looked guilty, but I never did. To make things work in the world, I had to be a little sneaky at times. The two of us just didn't meld. He would always want to hang out with me, but I never would.

Every day for 6th or 7th grade, in Catholic school, we had a story of a different saint. One saint that I remembered lived very spiritually as a child, but then went off and lived very hedonistically. In the end he came back and became one of the greatest saints of the church. I think it was St. Augustine. They read through that story, and I wanted to be just like that one.

My mom and father Charles at Charlie's Corner diner where my brother and I waited tables

Me at 15 years old and at 17 years old.

My mom Emma and Grandma Ciola in her Florida orange grove.

1950s

TEENS

I was very spiritual as a young child, but then I rebelled. I threw everything out. When I was in high school, all good Catholics were supposed to fast from eating meat every Friday. But, because it was something I wasn't supposed to do, I would sneak off and get a hamburger. I figured, "That's not God's law. Where the heck had *that* come from?" Soon I threw the whole religion out. I even questioned whether there really was someone called Jesus.

In high school, I didn't fit in. But I had a protector—Peter Shane the big, tough offensive guard on the football team. He befriended me. We had study hall together. Nobody gave me any trouble. If anyone ever tried to mess with me, Peter would take care of it—big time! One time somebody started to pick on me, and I said, "You know, you don't want Peter to hear about this." That stopped it instantly.

My father wanted me to be more manly. So, he talked to the coach, and for a year, they put me in as the manager of the football team. The team would have a football meeting during the last period of the school day. I didn't consider myself a real part of the team, so I wouldn't go. But the players would come and get me. They wanted me involved.

Then spring practice came at the end of the school year, and my father had pressured the coach again, you know, to make me even more manly. I just went along. So, they put a real football uniform on me to do the real football stuff. I *never* knew what was going on. I never knew what I was doing. We'd set up our practice—scrimmage, I think they called it. And the defensive player across from me would have to tell me what to do each time.

He'd say something like, "Now Charles, bump me, then head out and take a left." I certainly never knew what I was supposed to do.

One time the football players got ahold of some "blue" movies. We were all supposed to travel somewhere together, but the players were meeting ahead of time in someone's garage to see these blue movies. But they wouldn't let me see them. Instead, they waited to pick me up afterwards. Another time in New York City, I walked into my first porno flick and one of my friends immediately dragged me out, saying "You shouldn't be seeing this!" *I* never knew why everyone was so protective of me.

When I graduated from high school, and needed to get to junior college, there was no public transportation to get there, so my dad bought me a used car—a nice car, too. He had also bought himself a new-to-him used car, a Studebaker, and had retired his old car—just parked it to keep for parts. In about two weeks, I wrecked my new car, totally. Once I had wrecked mine, he gave me his Studebaker, and went back to driving his old, dilapidated jalopy, which by that time had no windows and no doors.

I graduated from high school in the spring of 1957. I spent two years at Palm Beach Junior College, through 1959. Then to the University of Florida, earning my degree in December of 1961.

The old, wreaked jalopy in front of my West Palm Beach childhood home

Landscaping, gardening, and plants runs in my blood. I come from a line of gardeners and farmers. My mother was Italian, my grandmother had a way with plants, and I ended up going to the University of Florida majoring in ornamental horticulture and landscape design. So, I actually have credentials to do what I ended up doing at the Meditation Retreat.

1960s

TEACHING WITHOUT THE TEXTBOOK

My first teaching job was right out of college. I taught four years in Miami, Florida, until 1967, then two years in Detroit, Michigan.

Did I tell you yet about the lesson plans? I needed a job—horticulture just doesn't pay as well as I needed right then—and someone said, "Why don't you try teaching?" And I said, "I could probably do that." Teaching in junior high—general biology. I had all the science qualifications, but none of the education courses. So, I went and applied for a teaching job in Miami. I had no teaching credentials, but I got this job.

You were required to make lesson plans. So, when I turned them in on Monday morning, my lesson plans would have one sentence, Tuesday, another sentence. The other teachers were doing 2 or 3 pages for a day, laying it all out, so their substitute teachers could follow through doing it. But I don't want my substitute teacher teaching my class. Let them read a book, or I'd give them things to do. But the assistant principal says to me, "These aren't adequate."

So I say, "Come into my class for a week, come in and out any time and then we'll talk." So, she did.

After seeing what we were doing, she says to me, "You can still hand in those one-sentence lesson plans. Just put 'em in a manila envelope so nobody else sees 'em." She saw what I was doing was actually working. And it was always different and fresh. What I said in the first class, I wouldn't say in the same way in the second class later in the day, even though it was just different students taking the same topic. The kids would come in for the fifth period class after having talked to those in the first period, and complain, "Aren't you going to tell us about the hamster?"

And I'd say, "No."

I'm right brained. I can't teach anybody's left-brained curriculum. I could show students how to solve a problem, but it would be a *right*-brained solution, not a left-brained solution.

I hadn't been there two weeks, and I got "remaindered." That means the newest teachers get bumped. They didn't have high enough enrollment. I had only been in that first school for two weeks, and now I was supposed to leave. They couldn't fire me. They were required to find another spot for me, but I wasn't going to be working *there*. The students passed around a petition to get me to stay "because I was meeting *their* needs rather than teaching some curriculum."

The principle called me in, and said they had an opening at a brand-new school, air-conditioned, state-of-the-art. He said, "You're going to get a lot of pressure from old-time teachers who would kill for an opportunity to transfer to a job like that. Don't let them talk you out of it. It's a prize position, and you should take it." I still didn't have a teaching credential!

In the new job, I had to teach biology, graphics for engineering, and remedial math. I had never been able to solve word problems! Well, the first day in remedial arithmetic, they are sweating about the word problem on the board. And I said, "Put your books away. I'm going to tell you how to solve this." Because I knew how to solve it, but not the way the textbook said of doing it. So we went through and solved all these problems, showing them a different way to do it.

The rest of the school was working on advanced biology, and I had been assigned to teach beginning biology to all the slow students. I was embarrassed by just how low an expectation the administration had for these students. So, I had them start to borrow their friends' advanced textbooks and had them reading particular chapters in them. Teachers weren't supposed to do that.

The borrowed texts were on molecular biology, which is all about chemistry. Well, I flunked my own chemistry class three times, because I've never been able to memorize, even using flash cards and all that. But I finally passed basic chemistry. And here I was teaching *advanced* chemistry. Later that year, a special course came to our county. They sent a teacher down to train how to teach this new course. And suddenly I was certified to teach advanced chemistry.

It's just an intuitive thing. That's how I got into all my professions at the top. Every couple years I would have a totally new profession. I never entered at the bottom, but ended up going in at the top and having to figure it out. I learned to trust my intuition. It's a little bit like having a library card to the Akashic Records![3]

AN INTUITIVE THING

The people in my family just knew things. Later in life I was living in New York City, I had quit my job and hadn't found a new one. I was talking to my mom, and less than 3 minutes into the conversation she suddenly asked, "How's work?" She never asked that before. She just knew.

Another time, I was talking to my brother, and he said, "Oh, you're coming down for a visit."

And I said, "There's no way. Whatever gave you that idea?"

"Oh," he said, "Mom had a dream."

"But there's no way I could get away now." But two weeks later there I was. My grandmother had died. And there I was. They just ... knew. It was an interesting childhood. All my aunts were tuned in that way.

I think that's where I got it. And I think later on that's why I got chosen to do this garden thing. Because I could hear inside, and I was willing to follow what I heard.

I once went to this party in a New York City high rise apartment. There were a lot of people there. I went in, but as soon as I went through the door, I *knew*. And I often say that "I heard," but this time it's more that, I *felt*. Like I felt parched in my throat. I don't know how to describe it, but I could tell there was a plant somewhere in that apartment needing water. It was as if there were someone out on the desert, dying from thirst. And I thought, "Well, I can't go get a drink for myself while that's going on!" If it had been a person there, I would have rushed to get him a glass of water first. And I walked all through this apartment until I found that plant and gave it the water it craved. And only then could I go on about enjoying that party. I couldn't do anything until I found that plant and helped it out of its pain. I was just born this way, even before I ever took any training in intuition.

At one point as a young man, I had a very successful houseplant business. I was big in the plant world. I did all the plants for the sunroom of the head people for American Express. I even wrote two books on houseplants for Random House. So, one day I was out in Southampton on Long Island, doing the plants for the owners of the huge motel and restaurant chain from the 70's, Howard Johnsons. They had a famous decorator working on the house. It got written up in Architectural Digest. And this decorator asked if I could help him by hanging this picture on the wall. So, I hung it for him. Then he asked me, "How did you know to put it exactly *there*?" Because it just *was* the right place. He begged me to come work for him. I wouldn't. But these are things I just knew.

I remember tramping in the Florida everglades with a group of about six guys. We were out collecting orchids for a Junior College botany class. You can get lost in the everglades because it's a savannah and these little islands all look the same. We were walking back, and I said, "This is not the right way." They started grumbling about why they should listen to me. Who was I, anyway? They just complained that I was leading them astray. So finally, I just say, "You know, you can go where you want, I'm going here."

So, I started to walk, and they followed along behind. And within 10 minutes we hit the road. I just knew. It's simply a talent. I listen inside, and most people mostly don't.

When I was living in Oregon, I had a cute little refrigerator. But the repairman said, "It can't be fixed."

I was a bit upset. So, I unplugged it and left it overnight. But the next morning I told it, "You're the right size, the right color—avocado green—where am I going to be able to find another one to go with the rest of my old kitchen?" The chance of finding another one and replacing it was not going to be easy.

So, I went over, plugged it in, and it worked!

And about every four or five months it would stop again, and I would unplug it, have a talk with it, plug it back in and it would work again. When I finally left Oregon for good, the fridge seized up, the stove blew up, and the well pump died. But for me, machines work.

I went up to Montreal for the 1967 world's fair with my mother. Every day I went with her to the fair. We did most of the exhibits backwards because she wasn't going to wait in any lines! We went in the back doors. I can remember going in the exit of the Soviet exhibit. It was scary. I thought, "We're gonna get shot!" It was at a time in history, the Cold War, when we didn't have great relations with them. There we were, just pushing past the guards and everything. We were up on the second floor, and one of the Kennedy's came in down below. She jumps across the rope, crawled under Sputnik, over to the balcony where she could look down and see Kennedy. I just knew we were going to get arrested.

After finishing my four-year teaching job in Miami, I got a job teaching in inner city Detroit for two school years, fall 1967 through spring 1969. Taking all my stuff from Florida to my new job in Detroit, I was driving a little rented U-Haul van. But it would only go 50-55 mph. I would get it going, and suddenly it would just peter out—no guts. After about an hour of this, I was going nuts. So, at a rest stop I pulled over, and looked under the hood at this motor. And I say to myself, "Whatever it is, I bet it's in here." I had no idea what I was pointing at. I took the lid off the thing—turned out to be the carburetor, I learned later—and there was a little contraption inside with a spring. And mucking around with it, I broke it. So, I went into the rest stop, got some Kleenex, and stuffed it in the thing to hold the valve open. It had been a governor, put there deliberately by the company to hold the speed down. And after that, with it propped open, I drove 65 mph. I don't know if they ever discovered that I'd stuffed Kleenex in there to overrule it. That once again was just having the chutzpah to go in there and do that.

Later, I was driving my old Land Cruiser that I had bought around 1990. It looked like it belonged on an African Safari, so I called it Bwana. If it was going to break down, it would never do so until it was right in front of an auto parts store.

I just had a relationship with these things. It all works together in life somehow. It's just an intuitive thing.

I was born with what I call pre-natal dementia. I almost got held back in the 4th grade because I couldn't remember my times tables. Basic chemistry I had to take 3 times before I could pass it. And then later I had to teach it! When I get up to the higher stuff, I know what to do. But it's the memorization of the lower stuff that gives me trouble. Being dyslexic[4] doesn't help.

My land cruiser named Bwana

That higher stuff I don't have to memorize, because I seem to have what I call a library card to the Akashic Record. And you have to hide that. It's not socially acceptable. It just makes you different. And you're not supposed to be different. So therefore, I just sort of stayed quiet.

To some extent, I guess it's about the right brain. It's the *left* brain that gets us all in trouble. But we need that left brain, too, because the right brain can't function on its own. People who can only use their right brain, we call airheads, or space cadets!

Yogananda's chauffeur Peggy Dietz tells a story about herself. At her very first meeting with the great yogi, he told her, "I could teach you how to leave your body consciously."

And Peggy immediately answered, "Oh Master, I do *that* all the time. What *I'm* trying to do is to stay *in* it!"

1970s

MATERIALISM EMBRACED

After four years teaching in Florida, I followed a friend to Detroit, and took an inner-city teaching job. But my life there didn't work out as well as I'd hoped, so two years later, in 1969, I moved to New York City. On many levels, my life really began after I moved to New York City.

I say that because *that's* when I had my first original thought, one that I recognized as being completely mine. It wasn't until I was 32 years old that I put something together in my head, and I go, "Wow." So, about 1971, I was no longer doing what everyone else expected. I was doing things that were new. And I like that excitement, that creative thing. There's a gene that they've discovered that's like an excitement gene. It causes you to seek more excitement, and it runs in families. It's like, if you have that gene and you have 3 kids, one of them will pick it up.

Most of the 70's for me was filled with a wild nightlife. It was high times. Oh, I had a terrific time. For instance, I was on the committee for the NPR fundraising auctions in New York City. They had a re-opening of the Copa Cabana nightclub, and I had complimentary ringside seats to the opening. I was in with all these rich, rich people on the committee—but *I* didn't have any money myself. It was all because my gallery was doing well, and I had a 3000 square foot apartment on Central Park West. I got it at a good price. Before that I had a ground floor garden apartment at Gramercy Park. All pretty swanky.

But even though those worldly times were interesting, you don't want to hear all those gory details. So, I'm going to skip to when the spiritual stuff started. In the late 70's, I was at our art gallery in New York City, in a prestigious location, and it was doing very well. I owned it, with two partners. I was pretty much the instigator. I actually made good money from it.

When I had the gallery, it was a gallery not of paintings, but of high-quality crafts--ceramics, batiks. It was the period, in the late 60's and early 70's, of the Cultural Revolution. Instead of going into the fine arts, young people went into the craft arts. Me and my partners gave these young craft artists a place where their work could be shown. We opened this gallery, and got all these artists, but we're running it all on consignment. And the artists weren't really into that. In the crafts world, they were used to people buying their stuff outright.

But I was able to talk them into it. Even now I have a fairly extensive vocabulary, though back then it was even bigger. In the gallery, some called me "the man with the silver tongue." I simply wouldn't stop talking until they gave me their work! I'd start by saying, "If you want your stuff here, this is how we're gonna do it," Then I'd say, "This is *not* two mugs for five bucks. We're dealing with art here, and you need to consign it." The craft artists that we got started in our gallery way back then are displayed nowadays in the Metropolitan Museum, and in major museums all around the world.

These painters or photographers would ask me, "Would you look at my work?" And I would answer, "Look around, do you see anything like yours here?" It wasn't what we were doing. We did crafts.

I was in the middle of painting the walls of our new gallery, and one of these people showed up. I'd have to stop what I was doing. This guy says, "You know, you've got a reputation of being able to see the artists' soul." And that I was the only one around like that they knew of. So occasionally I'd say, "OK." I wouldn't carry their product on our walls, but I'd at least set their work down, lean it against the wall, then I'd step back and look at it. And I'd talk to them about what I was seeing. And I'd look up, and they'd be crying. In their work all I was seeing was *them*.

Even without them being there, it's all there in the painting.

It used to amaze me how I could just take a couple of breaths, and I'd be a different person. I had to go deep inside because it was a privilege to look into someone's soul. You couldn't do that lightly.

Gala re-opening of the Copa Cabana nightclub to which I was invited in New York City

The pharaoh statue at the Karnak Temple Complex near Luxor, Egypt

EGYPT VISITED, JERUSALUM REVISITED

Some friends of mine had signed on for a tour package to Egypt. Ten days. I'd never been out of the country—never even had a passport. And I said, "I could do that." So, I got my passport quickly and signed on for this tour. And off we go to Egypt.

We were staying right outside of the pyramids. I kept feeling this should feel different to me. But it just felt natural. You see, I could remember being in Egypt. It didn't feel unusual at all. The only thing unusual was that man over there was repairing a roof and he was using his hands to spread the tar, and another was using palm fronds to sweep the street. I was starting to feel concerned that this wasn't feeling exotic. At that point in my life, I didn't yet know about past lives and stuff.

We spent time in the Great Pyramid. I hadn't done any research before I traveled. The only thing I did beforehand was play Paul Horn's flute album recorded inside the Great Pyramid. That was my only research.

But later we ended up at the Karnak Temple Complex near Luxor and went to the light show. Your mind fills in what's missing. There was this big voice over the loudspeaker talking in the first person. In this big open space with obelisks all around, one of our people passed out. Others were reviving him. Something kept pushing me on my chest, pushing me backwards, stumbling downhill a long city block then up some stairs. I had no idea what was happening, but at the same time I had no idea why I didn't totally freak. I had told myself earlier that when going to Egypt I would be a sponge, just trying to take it all in. I stood there feeling silly, as I thought to myself, "Be a sponge!"

Intrepidly, I walked back inside, but by the time I got back to the big courtyard, my whole group was gone. I was still "sponging." Something grabbed me by my shirt around the neck, pushing me backwards violently. Suddenly I found myself in front of this tall pharaoh statue, and between its legs was a smaller statue, I think it was his wife. So, I was looking at this statue, and all of a sudden, my head snapped back, and I got plugged into what felt like an electric circuit. My whole body just started shaking. But I still was not spooked. It was just energy coursing through me. Way off in the distance, I heard my name—my friends had finally missed me. I came out of it, though I was still in kind of a daze. But I certainly wasn't prepared to tell anybody about what I had felt.

I came back to the States. I was in the gallery. And I told a little bit of it to this lady there, and she told me about this psychic training coming up soon. So, I took this psychic awareness course in New York City in 1978. Michael Crichton, the author of Jurassic Park, was there. It had really turned his attitudes around. He had been quite a skeptic. That course was an important steppingstone for me. It was right about the time for me that the worldly changed toward the spiritual. One man in the class named Keith made me very nervous. I just couldn't stand being around him. Keith would come into the room, and I would have to leave. The day before our graduation, I had this vivid dream about him. In feudal Japan, he had cut off my head, just out of jealousy. Next day at the graduation party, he came up to me with a tear in his eye and said, "I cut off your head!" He had had the same dream.

So, I looked at him, and said, "OK, Keith, just don't do it again!" At that point, we had cleared the air between us. There had been no way until that dream that either of us could have understood what had been going on. Best we could do—just like if you're holding a hot rock in your palm—is let it go! Awareness might come later, as it did this time about my antipathy[5] toward Keith.

In the psychic awareness course, we were studying past lives. One technique was to lie down, relax, and they would give you directions about going in and out of your body. I thought it was ridiculous, so I started making up all this stuff.

Then they said, "Come out of your body. Now when you go back in, it will be in one of your past lives." Instantly they threw more questions at me: "What are you wearing on your feet?" And I was wearing sandals, very dusty. "And what clothes are you wearing?" Oh, a skirt. And then they asked, "Where are you?" And always before this time I'd been making it up. But somehow now I'd connected. I would never have gone there in a million years—not in a million years. That was nowhere near anything in my conscious thinking.

I was in Jerusalem. I was aware that it was happening. I had bumped into Jesus at the Sermon on the Mount—sorry, I always get a little emotional here—but right then I realized I was at the crucifixion. All that I could tell was I was there. I was one of the Roman soldiers that were keeping an eye on Jesus and the crowds that had gathered around him.

Obviously, lying there on the floor in the psychic awareness course, I had connected, but now I was growling in severe stress. They asked me, "Do you want to come out of it?"

But I couldn't speak. All I could get out was, "They're killing him!" I was a Roman soldier saying this.

And then they asked me, "How did you die?" Being a soldier with my new beliefs, I had been punished by being posted far out in the wilderness. And now I had this huge sword, a big wide thing, stuck in my gut. And then there was Jesus. And he lifted me clear out of my body.

I have never had a substantial fear since then. After that, everything else paled. Before, I had gotten myself into the mindset of a Christ-denier. But never again. And never since have I been interested in past lives as a party thing. I thought that would be abusing these truths. It would be like charging for spirituality. You've got to be very careful. It's a thin line.

Actually, my very first past life remembrance had been way back in 1972 or '73. I had one of those momentary flashbacks, when I had been somewhere else. I knew who I was, where I was, what it looked like, what it felt like, what it smelled like. It was in England, long ago. At the time I felt all this, I attributed it to my Welsh/Irish heritage on my father's side, genetically, but now I feel confident that it had been one of my past lives. I had been the mayor. I don't know what my title was exactly, but there was something of importance about it. The realization only lasted a second, but all of this got communicated during that brief moment. Even when you play Bharat Cornell 's[6] nature games, and you do that Camera Game of his, it only lasts a few seconds, but it's all engrained. It's still in there. I can still describe to you everything that I wore in that past life. The image came full-blown. That's how you sort of know that it's real because it all comes in. You are not having to imagine it. That's what blew me away with the crucifixion story. It wasn't something that I was making up, it was something that I was feeling, and it affected me so deeply and so permanently.

They sure are nice touches that the Divine gives us, sometimes! What if some people don't seem to get these intuitions? I'm sure we all do, of one type or another. Not just past life knowings. Those are just one type of touch the Divine can give us.

Over time in the Retreat garden, I think I've discovered some truths. When we die, the brain, the thing that creates intellect, goes. It rots. Gone forever. In that sense, the atheists are correct. There *is* only one life for this intellect. We don't carry that with us later. But what we *do* carry with us is all the emotion stuff, the love, and the fear, because there's no intellect left later on. That's why it's so hard for us to remember from one life to another. We remember, but we can't put the words to it, because it's not there in the intellect. We remember the feelings, but not the words. Like the story about Keith cutting off my head in a past life, the feeling was there, but no story was attached to it in my mind until I got the dream. Getting more and more in touch with our feeling side, and riding it like a surfboard, I believe we can figure out more about our past lives.

Both the Egypt trip, and the psychic awareness course, were really the beginning—the switching from the worldly to the spiritual. I'd been taking all these psychic courses and having all these phenomena. I continued with my spiritual searches, began investigating New Age stuff, and the worldly stuff began to wane.

Every once in a while, I would ask a psychic, "Do I have a guru?"

And they'd say, "Yes, he's on the other side." And I'd always say, "Well, a lot of good that's going to do me!" During this psychic course time, 1978, I read *Autobiography of a Yogi*, and at the end of reading that book, I just cried, because Yogananda was dead. I wouldn't have taken a bus to meet Yogananda like Swamiji did—I would have chartered an airplane! I knew he was the only one—I wasn't going to find any other—it was *him*.

I had a summer place out at the beach on Fire Island. I would go out every Sunday evening and Monday, and I would move away from where the people were, and just sit, and write poetry. Very inward; a very special time. And I would just talk to the water and ask it if I could come in. Sometimes it would say yes, and sometimes no. One particular day in August 1978—it was my birthday—instead of going away from the people this time, I said, "I'll stay near where the people are." There was a big hump of sand away from the water, and behind that is where I had left my towel. The waves were rough that day. And I went to the water's edge and asked. I was being very woo-woo. And I got, "No." I went back to my towel, and was reading my book in the sun.

Suddenly, this big tongue of water came up over this bluff and engulfed me. I'm grabbing my book and my glasses and my blanket and everything. I look around and I'm the only one. The water had come up to nobody else. Now, my towel was full of sand, so I went down to the water's edge to rinse off my towel, and there were people out playing in the waves. It looked very inviting.

I took my towel back by the bluff, then returned to the water's edge. I'm not the best to be in deep water. My lungs were affected long ago by polio, and the water puts pressure on my chest, so it makes it tough to breathe. And again, suddenly, another wave caught me. They weren't breaking in just one place, but chaotically. It caught me, and I started to tumble. I must have left my body, because I saw myself tumbling, and everything was light. I heard about this way of describing it later on, but now that's exactly what I saw. Everything was light. The water at this seashore was not clear. But while I was out of my body, it was perfectly clear. The bottom was glistening sand, and the surface was like a mirror. Here's Charles, tumbling in all the bubbles. I'm out there, feeling no pain. And then this voice says, "How poetic Charles, on your birthday. Get back in there!" And all of a sudden, I was gulping, and spitting, and drowning! All the sensations of drowning were back, and people on shore had seen it, and had formed a human chain to grab me, and pull me back onto shore.

MATERIALISM RENOUNCED

Up until the Egypt trip and the psychic course, I'd had a terrific time, really the high life. And I always had nice stuff. It just comes. But I always told myself that I wasn't attached to it.

Then we had a great recession in late 1978-79. And suddenly money just dried up.

While I was staying out at my beach place, I had taken a friend who needed a place to stay into my 3000 square foot town apartment. And he had abused staying there so badly, that I got kicked out. It had been a very nice place. I had had an option to buy the place outright for $53,000. In 2013 the same place sold for $7 million. Later, I remember thinking, "I could love God just as well if I were rich," but obviously God didn't agree.

While I was in the big place, getting kicked out, I started to smell sulfur, and things seemed murky. It was clear only as far out as my arm could reach. I was pretty paranoid. I could almost feel vultures flying overhead. Right then, in December of 1978, people from the Mafia came into my life with great temptations, and told me, "You don't have to go. We can get you this apartment, then we can move you to an even better apartment." They thought I would make a good front man for them.

Now, I was sort of curious. So, I went to 3 meetings. But I knew it was a bit like Tar Baby in the Uncle Remus stories. How do you get yourself back out once you get started in something like this? So, there I am meeting with the Mafioso types. And I ask, "So how are you going to do this?"

And they said, "Roy Cohn, do you know who he is?" He was the guy that McCarthy used as one of the attorneys in the anti-communist hearings—a very corrupt man. They said, "He 'owns' 50% of the judges in NYC. So, we can get anything we want." Roy's right-hand man during those hearings had been Richard Nixon.

It was time to get out of this. Two of the Mafioso types and this big black bodyguard said they were going to the gym, and they would give me a ride to where I lived. We were in the elevator, and the black guy was bouncing a basketball, and all of a sudden, he palmed it, and he said, "Bet you can't do that?"

And I said, "How much? Want to make a bet? How about ten dollars?"

"Ya, you can't do that. I'll bet you ten dollars."

So, I bounce once, twice, three times, then boink! "You mean that?" I don't know how, but it stuck to my hand.

He says, "I don't see no white man can do that."

We got in their big limo, and pulled up to my corner, and I turned around and I said, "I want my $10. We had a bet. I want my $10." And I throw a big hissy fit.

The black guy says, "I only got a $100 bill."

Well, that day someone had given me $100, and I had bought some gum or something. "I've got change!" I never heard from them again.

When I got home, I looked around me and said, "You know, it's all this *stuff*." I'd always said I wasn't attached to the stuff. "I bet it's about all this stuff." So, I just called all my friends and said I'm selling everything. I left that apartment with just two suitcases, and the owners ended up giving me $15,000, because I had done some renovations for the owner. And I made another $15,000 in selling all my stuff. People were coming out of the woodwork to buy my stuff. So, I made out very well. And in January of 1979 I just walked away from that old lifestyle.

PILGRIMAGE TO INDIA

During this process, I had taken an EST-type course called Actualizations. They taught that if you ever get backed up against a wall, there is only one question to ask yourself: "What's the most ludicrous thing you could do? And do it."

So, I'm walking down to the subway, heading to work, and I'd remembered that advice. This is really one of those times when I'm really up against it—I even had to borrow those 50 cents to get to work. So, I asked, "What's the most ludicrous thing you could do?" I answered, "Go around the world!" Well, that certainly seemed ludicrous.

From that, I ended up buying a one-way ticket to India. People kept asking, "Why are you going to India?"

I'd say, "I don't know. They speak English." I had never had any desire to go to Europe. So, I ended up spending six months traveling around in India. And when I finally came home, I made sure that I came home in such a direction that it turned out I had traveled all the way around the world.

So, in 1979 that took me to India. But while I was there, I wouldn't go anywhere near an ashram. I would go to the temples. And there was always a guy who wanted to give you the grand tour. Of course, there often was a sign that said, "Hindus only", and I'm not a Hindu. But it mostly worked. I was sponging, trying to take it all in. This is the right way to travel when you're like me, and not particularly fond of talking with strangers.

I found I had a prejudice against India—something like that British Raj looking-down-at-incompetence kind of thing. That was a surprise to me that I had that prejudice. I was raised not to have prejudices. It just wasn't allowed growing up in my household. So, I wasn't connecting with the locals, rather I was just looking and absorbing. I knew I didn't want this prejudice to remain, but it took quite a bit of time to get rid of it.

I'd only been in India for less than a week. But I had a particularly special experience in the small temple village of Pushkar, about eight miles by bus from Ajmer, Rajasthan.

Pushkar is a holy city, out in the Rajasthani desert, surrounding a lake about the size of two football fields. There are bathing ghats, or steps, all the way around the lake where people bathe daily and spill the ashes of their cremated loved ones into the lake. This lake is considered holy just like the Ganges River. The town contains the only temple in all of India dedicated to the aspect of God known as Brahma.

This little old man befriended me. I'm not that interested in talking much, because so often with their accents I can't understand what they're saying—it's just too difficult. He didn't press it. But we went into a ruined house, which is now a fancy hotel, and went to the edge of Lake Pushkar, and sat on the ghat. Another way to think about the lake's size is about eight times larger than the Ananda Village's Lotus Lake. And I dreamed of staying there forever, and remodeling this house, taking in tourists.

It was Puja time in the evening. Pushkar has 500 temples, so there were all these bells clanking. Plus, there were children splashing and playing in the water, and giggling and laughing. It just became a symphony. It took me someplace else. It just stole my heart. I can't tell you why. It's just a feeling.

This man had some kids run off and bring me a gift, a Krishna statue. Now normally when the Indians are through with their statues, they throw them in the lake. But this Krishna and I had a very strong connection. Like we knew each other, there was something that passed between us. So, to this day I still have *this* Krishna statue in my home. Finally, he was taking me back to catch the bus. And I heard kettle drums. And he says, "Puja!" And he takes me down this alley. We get to this courtyard, and up on the second story, there was a balcony, and an Indian priest, doing a puja. A big heavy man, mustache, turban, with 3 helpers doing the puja with him. There was a woman hunched over in the dark sitting on the stairs that led up to the balcony. There was a lamp, and the pujari doing all this stuff, then using the lamp for blessing everyone and everything out beyond the balcony.

And then my little host takes ahold of my arm, drags me up the stairs, and pushes me into the middle of this puja. I had no idea what was going on. I was raised Catholic! Pushing my hands toward the fire, blowing a conch in one of my ears, throwing water at me, ringing a bell in my other ear.

My kundalini just let go. I spiraled right out of the body. I didn't go far—I was very conscious of it—just about cloud height. I thought, "Boy, this is strange." Then I zoomed back down, but I was totally, totally disoriented with the power of sound. They had to help me back down the steps, and onto the bus.

There was another lesson like this one about how ritual and sound can affect us. I was up in Dharamshala where the Tibetan monks growl as their spiritual practice. To me, what they're doing with their deep chanting and their clanking noises, it seems like they're opening portals into another dimension, getting what they need, or adding what they need, and then coming back out. The clank is the sound of the portal closing again. It can be a bit annoying with all that noise. It certainly isn't my path, but all this helped me recognize that other people's paths work, too.

I spent a whole month in Kashmir. I could have stayed there forever. It was one of the most beautiful places I have ever been. I stayed out on Lake Nigeen on a houseboat called "The Ritz." It was an old Raj era houseboat. I didn't want one of the new ones. And I kept getting drawn by something on the other side of the hill. There was this big hill that up on top had structures that were falling apart. I kept getting drawn to that. So, I borrowed the little boat called a shikara one day and paddled across and walked up this hill—which I'm not inclined to do. I don't walk up hills well because of the polio I got as a kid. And up to the top, there were interesting ruins—I like ruins—you get to feel like I'd experienced in that Psychic Course. And I get over to the edge and am drawn down the backside of this hill—just drawn down. I just wanted to run down this hill, to this town that was down there. But I didn't, because then I would have to climb back up. And I had no idea where that was because it was around the other side of the mountains. Come to find out that was the tomb where, some claim, Jesus was buried. It had been just like a magnet.

Another interesting thing took place while I was out in the Rajasthani desert near Ajmer. Once again, I started to walk up a mountain. This was a big thing, the trail all zig-zaggy. I was just intending to walk a little way, but I got into it and felt drawn up the hill. I came across a man carrying two big five-gallon buckets of water hanging from each end of a yoke balanced over his shoulder. There was no water up on the top of the hill. I talked to him a little bit, gave him my pack and carried up his load of water buckets a ways. I got past one switchback, then said, "OK, that's enough." Then I gave him back his water buckets and continued to the top. On the top was a Sufi saint's tomb. The sun was setting. The full moon was rising. It was phenomenal. I was almost ecstatic from the beauty. I remember saying, "You know, I don't know what's going on. I know You're trying to tell me something, but I can't figure it out. I've never been good at this abstract stuff. I have never understood Fellini movies. I have no idea what You're trying to tell me." Then I cried out, "English. You need to speak in English!" Nothing. No response. Not a thing!

So next I traveled further into Rajasthan. I kept getting dysentery. Terrible, terrible dysentery. I'd kept making myself—well there was no choice—eating this Indian food, with all its chilis. I got so weak I thought I was going to die. I got all the way out to Jaisalmer. The last straw was taking a nine-hour bus ride across the desert, with dysentery, squatting on this seat with the bolts coming up through the padding, and the window unable to close, and right behind the driver who was coughing and hacking with phlegm. Then he would spit one of those big luegies that would go out and immediately get pushed by the wind right back in my open window. I had a scarf, so every time he started hacking, in self-defense I would cover the window with the scarf; nine hours of this. We finally got to Bikaner. I threw the scarf away, and checked into a hotel to sleep an hour or two.

I figured if I didn't get back to Delhi soon, I was going to die. So, I went down to the train station and tried to buy a ticket to Delhi. But there were no tickets. In those days you couldn't just walk into an Indian train station and get a ticket. Sometimes it took a couple of days. But the ticket master behind the window inquired, "Good sir, where are you from?" I said, USA. "But what city are you from?" I said, New York City. "Oh, sir, I have a brother in New York City!"

And I said to myself, "I have a ticket!" I felt a little guilty because I knew I was working him, but he found me a ticket.

He put me in first class, in the compartment that already had a senator in it. When the senator showed up—you know how haughty Indian politicians can be—he was completely incensed that I was in his compartment. But I was not feeling well. And I wasn't going to take any grief. He had his manservant who slept outside the door. It came time to get to bed, the senator said he wanted the bottom bunk. But I said with full energy, "I was here first!" He was a big fat man. Finally, I conceded, and I gave him the bottom and I took the top.

I knew that I had to eat before I got on the train, because the train food is worse than the street food—way too much cayenne. I didn't really understand yet what was happening in my gut, because I'd only been there a month. So I went and ordered some food. I took one bite and went into convulsions, shaking. This booming voice, sounding to me like it was in an echo chamber, said, "You fool. It's the chilis!"

And I can remember thinking, "It's in English!" Finally, I had some direction I could follow! So that's how I learned I was allergic to chilis.

I got down to 140 pounds not eating chilis. Couldn't eat *anything* in India. Only potatoes. Even the stuff they swore had no chilis in it, even that was cooked in pans that still had chili oil on them. So I had a lot of toast—toast and poached eggs and potatoes.

I stayed in several places in India that I positively recognized from past lives. Across the ocean in Sri Lanka, the Botanical Gardens was one place I almost went into bliss. And Madras, what they now call Chennai. I had to wait there for a friend who was coming over—for ten days I never left my hotel. I never went farther than the entrance door to the hotel, where I would buy mangoes, bring them back to the room and put them in the top of the toilet tank to cool them off. But I never went anywhere. I felt almost suffocated in Madres. But I had taken that Psychic Awareness Course, so I knew that something not very good must have happened there. There were also times in Rajasthan when I could see myself there in the past. I went from the top to the bottom of India, around the bottom tip, even over to Sri Lanka, six months.

That's really where my celibacy took hold. During those three black days in New York City when the sulfur and the vultures felt like they were flying around, I had decided, "You know, I've had enough of this." Been there, done that. I've always been very curious. There is very little that I haven't done. In India, I declared myself "quasi-celibate," because I knew I couldn't trust that I would stay celibate forever. In case an amazing opportunity came up, I might not have the energy to hold it off. I was 39. I said to myself, "You know, everything from this point on is going to be redundant, and Charles, you do not like redundancy." I don't even like to walk the same way two days in a row.

I can't say that I've been strictly celibate, but this was the beginning. In 1979 in India, it was total. Not even the desire. But even until this day, when I'm 85, I still think about it, that desire pops in. Like an alcoholic on his deathbed saying I want a drink. But I'm able to say "no." It is no longer the main event of my life. But it amazes me still—those feelings drag on, even though it seems ridiculous.

Upon traveling back to the U.S. from India, I flew into San Francisco, got off the plane, and stepped onto the bus at the street corner. After spending six months in India, I was amazed—everything was so clean! I was completely confused. There was no rickshaw to take me to the hotel! I didn't know what to do. But there was a phone booth, and I had a phone number of a woman I had met up in Kashmir, named Jan. We had bonded right away. I called the number, and her boyfriend answered the phone. Unfortunately, she wasn't there. She was off at a meeting. I had nowhere else to stay. So, I said, "If Jan had been here, she would have wanted me to come there!" So, he told me how to get there, and I went.

So, he asked me, "What would you want to eat tonight?"

And after six long months with Indian food, I cried out, "Pizza!" So, we went out and had pizza. And I stayed with Jan and her boyfriend for a month and a half. That was in the Haight Ashbury.

The holy city of Pushkar, Rajasthan with its bathing ghats and 500 temples

Me and my dear friend Meris Blumstein in her Manhattan apartment

Me in New York City in my 40's

1980s

GAP YEAR

After that, I headed back to the East Coast. I borrowed a house from some friends—the Blumstein's—who are as close to me as my own family. They had a house in the Delaware Water Gap in New Jersey. That's a valley the Delaware River runs through before the river goes through Philadelphia. I borrowed the house for the winter of 1979-80, sorting my slides. (In India, I had taken 3000 of them.) I had some nice revelations in that house, processing what this India trip was all about.

The house was a little summer getaway place that an Italian Count had built years ago for his mistress who worked at the U.N. I had been completely celibate for a long time now, the whole time I'd been over in India. But there was so much sexual energy in that house. That's how the Count had used the place. They had their little trysts there.

The house was completely unconnected with the real world. I don't even think there was a phone. I was disconnected from people everywhere. So, I really needed a mailbox. It wasn't easy to get one, though, because I had no car. It was over three miles to the closest town, and I'm not much of a walker because of my childhood polio. There was no local bus, so I had to wait until someone visited, then I had them drive me to town. I bought the mailbox, painted it up nice, took it down the hill to the road, dug the hole, put the box up, and trudged back up the hill.

The next day, I had to walk to town to get groceries. And I'm going down the hill and I'm all excited that I'm going to see my mailbox. And it's gone! My mailbox is gone. I felt so isolated and lost, like somebody had just cut my umbilical cord. I'm just bawling. I have to get to town because I needed food. I'm walking to town, and I'm thinking, "You know, a little bit down the way this is gonna be funny. What about now?" So, I'd laugh a little bit, then I'd cry a little bit. Then I'd laugh at me crying. Then I'd cry at my laughing. And I passed a garbage dump, and I'd think, "This is one of the most beautiful things I've ever seen." That was a big realization that there's beauty in everything. Non-beauty is a relative thing. We humans add that to what is true.

It took me a couple of weeks to get another mailbox. I went into the post office crying, "They stole my mailbox." Someone had just liked it and decided to take it. I had made it very pretty. This is what back country areas

Teresina and Joe Haven at the Temenos Retreat near Amherst, Massachusetts

can be like. Early Ananda Village always had that problem. For years they couldn't keep a mailbox standing along Tyler Foote Rd. It became a sport for somebody. Every time we would rebuild it stronger, they would come along and try their best to destroy it. After 3-4 months, I was told my friends, the Blumsteins, were selling that Delaware Water Gap house, so I had to move on. I didn't know where to go.

Teresina

FINDHORN AND BUDDHISM

In the summer of 1980, a friend came by with a brochure about a place called the Sirius community, which is a Findhorn community near Amherst, Massachusetts. They sign their letters, "Siriusly Yours." The founders of this place were trained right at Findhorn.

Findhorn is a community in Scotland where the nature spirits had a message for mankind and were able to communicate to this group of people. For a period of time, the nature spirits gave nice long messages. I always recommend the book called *The Findhorn Garden* book to anybody that hasn't read it. It's full of heart messages from nature, to help mankind get through this time.

Here's one little story from Findhorn. One time they wanted to put in a garden, and there were a bunch of brambles, like blackberries. So, the gardeners sat down and meditated. The nature spirits were working with them. Then, the Findhorn gardeners asked, "Can we take you out? We want to put in this nice garden, and perhaps a rose garden or something . . ." And the answer came back in their meditation, "No, no, no!" And the gardeners were surprised because they had always gotten affirmative answers before this. And the plants answered, "No, no, no, not now. We're about ready to bloom. That's how we praise God." So, whenever you see plants blooming and flowering, that's what they're doing. By listening, and talking to it, you sort of become one with nature. That's what Findhorn teaches.

One of the lines in the brochure for the Sirius community said, "If you think you should be here, come!" So, I dialed the phone. And said, "I think I should be there." I wasn't there very long. It was all very strange because I'm trained in science and traditional horticulture. They don't plant their foods in straight rows. They plant in funny little circles, and they're meditating all the time, morning, noon, and night. So, I'm doing all of this. I was there a couple of months.

Soon the Sirius people went to a networking conference, with all the alternative-types—the Rainbow People, the social activists, etc. So, I went along with them, and while I was there, I just couldn't take my eyes off this old woman who was there. She walked about with two sticks—she was old, and her hips were bad. My gaze was glued onto her. But I was shy, so I wouldn't talk to her. But I would follow her. I would stand behind a post and peek around. I couldn't take my eyes off her. I was stalking her. I would listen to her talk. I was just mesmerized, totally in love. I asked, "Who *is* she?"

My Sirius friends told me, "That's Teresina Haven. She and her husband have a little retreat place about 6 miles from us." So, a few days later, I had them drop me off at the bottom of this mountain called Mt. Mineral, in Shutesbury, near Amherst, Massachusetts. And I walked uphill on this road. Near the top hung an old tire rim, a stick to hit it with, and a sign that said, "Hit this two times for each season." So, I go gong gong, gong gong, gong gong on the rim. And I'm just blown away. It was a *very* powerful spot. I get up to the top, and I see Teresina. She's by this little pond, and I ask her, "What's the significance of the bell?"

"That's so I can get dressed, I don't know you well enough yet! So, what do you want?"

"Nothing."

She shouts, "Joe, Joe, get over here. There's a young man over here who wants nothing!"

They were Buddhist Quakers. Temenos was a primitive place. No electricity. No running water. We drew our water from a well. We didn't even have propane lights, but kerosene lanterns. Very similar to the way Ananda's Meditation Retreat was when it first started. Sacred ground. Temenos was on the site of an old mineral springs healing hotel that had burnt down. It had a couple of cabins. The mineral springs were still there. So, I moved in a week later. I ended up helping them build their lodge.

Mindfulness and consensus were their two most important principles. I never really got on with her husband. I do tend to gravitate to the women. Joe was a Jungian psychologist, and he was a bit of an authoritarian figure, and I wasn't going to have any of that. But *her* I adored. I stayed there because of her. I was there that summer, and a total of three consecutive complete summers. By "complete" I mean the entire time the weather was warm, so from about April through September. But in the winters, I had to find somewhere else to go. I would go into Northampton and rent a little place. They stayed on the mountain in the winters, but their cabin had better facilities, propane tanks and such. There was no way to winter over in the other cabins.

After two extended summers at Temenos, most of 1980 and '81, I was in this new cabin that was being built, that they named "Pine Cabin." They hadn't put windows in it yet. We *had* put screens in, so it was wonderful in the summer. But now it was getting to be October '81 and it was cold up in the mountains—these were the Berkshires, after all. I remember sleeping under every blanket that I had, plus I kept my hat on. I would go to this overlook and look out over some more mountains. And every day there I'd say, "I need some guidance. I need to know where to go. It's getting cold. And I need *someplace* to go." I knew this was a big one I was asking. "Just give me some guidance. I'll go anywhere *but* New York City." After asking this same question day after day, and getting no answer, finally one day it just dawned on me, "It is New York City, isn't it?"

"OK, I'll *do* it. But only under protest!"

INTUITION AT WORK

While I was still up at Temenos, a lady's car wouldn't start. So, the hood was up. All the guys were around, acting real macho, tinkering with this, and tinkering with that. Little dumb me, I'm sitting there looking at it. And I pointed to something under the hood and meekly offered, "The trouble is in *there*!" They looked at me like I was crazy. Soon they realized they couldn't solve the problem and had to call the mechanic. The mechanic came over. It turned out it *was* in that thing. It was a rotor or something in there that had gone bad. I was just born with that—good intuition. That's what got me through all these different jobs.

Sometime in the early 1980's, I had an epiphany, a bit like when Yogananda saw the spiritual structure that tied all of Omar Khayyam's *Rubaiyat* together. By now, I'd been back for years from my first trip to India. And I was already on the spiritual quest. I was walking up Madison Avenue, and I had one of those ah-ha moments when the light bulb goes on in the brain.

I had gone through India totally naïve. I don't tend to study before doing something. Like that teaching job I had. One astrologer told me I had many Jewish past lives. I must have carried the chutzpah forward. Previously, to me, Hinduism had always seemed to just be about pagans and idols. I had never had any inclination toward Hinduism. I had been more Buddhist by temperament. I hadn't run into any Hindu things other than the Hari Krishnas, and they had always seemed strange to me.

So, I was walking up Madison Ave. Ever since I had gone to India, everything I saw reminded me of something I had seen in India. A sunset, the color of a building. It was continuous. At that point it was just part of my being. I must have been subconsciously mulling over this six-month trip. I had gone as a sponge. And now I was starting to wring it out. Hinduism to me had just been a pagan mishmash. Who could figure it out?

Suddenly, I stopped in my tracks. There was a light involved with it, like a flash, a brightness. And suddenly I realized that I understood—at least the basics of— Hinduism. I remember saying to myself, "Oh, *that's* what it's all about!" It all came together. It all sort of jived. I can't initiate any conversations about it verbally, but I can usually add to discussions about it. So, it's in there.

After the guidance that said that I was supposed to go back to New York City, in late 1981 I went "back into the Lion's Den." When I got back to the City, I stayed with friends, and apartment sat. I needed to work, because all my money was gone. I got a lead from a friend of mine that they needed an expeditor at the UN Plaza Hotel restaurant. So, I went and applied for this job, and got it, because I have a good eye. My job was to check the food as it went out to make sure it was up to par. This is a four- or five-star hotel across from the U.N. Of course, I didn't have the actual experience to qualify for such a job. I did grow up while my father had a restaurant and I had learned how to cook a bit, but this wasn't a cooking job. I made the toast, warmed the croissants, and put them on the plates, making sure everything was arranged nicely before it went out. And at lunchtime I checked all the food that was going out, because they were having trouble with the appetizers and the salads and those kinds of things. That was an important part of the restaurant's presentation since those items were what went out first.

I ended up having to re-make most of the food, because the person behind the counter was a real slob--dirty fingernails. One day I said, "Alex, this is not satisfactory. This is smoked salmon. You're supposed to be able to read a newspaper through it. It's not supposed to come out in chunks. Give me that damn fish and give me a knife." I didn't know how to do it, but I knew how it ought to look. So, I laid it all out.

After a while, the food and beverage manager says to me, "Charlie, you're remaking all this food anyway, I want you in the kitchen." Sure, I'm doing it anyway. I thought all I had to do was plate it up. Up until now, I had been dressed in regular clothes all the time, because I'm behind the scenes.

But all of a sudden, they give me this outfit I have to wear. The checkered pants, the white smock, the tall hat. I had to get dressed down in the locker room, which was sort of creepy for me. I'm told a recent past life was a royal one, so some of that prejudice comes across. Was I going to have to change clothes with *these* people? That's the same place where my prejudice in India came from. So, at the hotel I got my little outfit on, and walk into the kitchen. The chef across the room throws me this two-and-a-half-foot long fish—this big salmon. And he says, "Charlie, poach this salmon."

I said to myself, "Oh my God, I have to cook this food. I had said yes because I thought I only had to make the food *beautiful!*"

So, I had to fillet it. My father had been a butcher, but I had not had a very good relationship with him. There were times I had said things. When my father and mother decided to divorce, I was overjoyed. My brother would try to get me to talk to my father—he was an alcoholic—but I wanted nothing to do with him. Finally, I worked it through enough that I could say, "OK, I can forgive him. You know, it takes two to tango," meaning both my father and my mother. My mother was a Scorpio, and he was Pisces. She just overpowered him, and he couldn't stand confrontation. "Now I can see it all, so I'll forgive him."

Then a little bit later, I just turned icy cold, as I heard from within, "How dare you even think that you have to forgive this man who sacrificed his whole life for you! You never wanted for anything! It was a total sacrifice." It wasn't until this moment in my mid-40s that I finally understood how much my father *had* loved me.

But here I was at the U.N. Plaza with this salmon. I had never watched my father butcher anything. But I had bought all the right knives for this job. So, I called out mentally, "Pop?" and my dad came. I knew what to do. I got guidance from my father. I filleted that fish perfectly.

Then I looked at one of the cooks across the counter, and I said, "You know, I *know* how to poach a salmon, but how do you do it *here*?" All these people had gone through years of training to get where they were. So, he told me, and I did it. It was a neat way to poach it. We wrapped it in saran wrap—plastic wrap—and popped it in the oven with Knox gelatin.

Then I had to make the potato salad, and the flan. And no one ever knew that I hadn't had any training, because my Pop was there for me all the time. It turned out to be a very important job for me for the next two years. While in that kitchen, I just automatically knew how to do things. I do cook at home, but you don't make a five-gallon bucket of potato salad at home. And there were definite recipes you had to follow, because it was the cuisine of the hotel. I would look in the mirror, and I was even starting to dress like my father. At the thrift store, I would be trying things on, not knowing consciously, and suddenly I realized: "*Dad* had that shirt." He's been with me ever since. That's why I can cook—I oversaw the kitchen here at the Meditation Retreat for a year. I knew how to do that because he was *there*.

But then two years had gone by cooking at the U.N. Plaza Hotel, and this one morning, I started to walk toward the door to go to work. But my feet wouldn't come off the floor. Just like what happened to Master right before he found his guru. I could lift my feet, but it felt like they had concrete blocks attached to them. And I think, "This is strange?" I don't know why I don't freak out when these things happen. I tried to move them a couple different times, and they just wouldn't go. But I felt fine. I didn't have any other symptoms. I could turn around and I could walk the other way, which I did, thinking if I walked the other way to get some momentum, then I'd be able to walk out the door. So, I tried that, but as soon as I turned the direction to go out, my feet wouldn't come off the ground again. I thought, "Well, I have to call in sick." I could walk to the phone, so I called in sick. Immediately after that, I was completely fine. I could go out the door. So, I went to the park and read. I had a nice day. I had no other symptoms. Next day, the same thing. Third day, the same thing. Fourth day, I said to myself, "OK, I think I've got it. I think you're having what they call 'burn out.' You hear them talking about this. This must be the symptoms of a burn out." So, I said, "You've got to go to work today, and you're going there in order to quit." So, I got dressed, and I was able to go.

I got to the subway. But when I got to Grand Central Station, I started to break into a sweat. To walk that block and a half to the U.N. Plaza Hotel, I had to concentrate hard to make my muscles work. I got to the door, and I could barely make the door open to go in. And the executive chef said, "Charlie, you're late!"

And I say, "I need to talk to you." So I went to his office, and I say, "I think I have this thing called burn out."

And he said, "We can understand that. And we're hoping you can give us the customary two weeks' notice." I just broke down and cried.

"I was hoping maybe you would send me home now?" At least I did have two helpers, so all day long the boss made me stand there and direct them. Hardest two days in my whole life. I just wanted to bolt—to get to the river and swim across and get out of there. Two days. But that was all I could do!

U.N. Plaza Hotel (the low brown one) across the street from the U.N., where I was chef

The new-age New York Open Center where I was hired as the janitor

IMPROBABLE JOBS, IMPROBABLE HOUSING

So sometime in 1984 I'd just been walking the streets, dejected. No job, money running low again. And I'm just talking to Divine Mother, saying, "I don't know what to do. I'm at the end of my rope. I really need help!" I was probably even crying.

I walk another block, and I bumped into these old acquaintances. "We were just talking about you. We need a business consultant. Would you agree to do that?" So, I took this job for a clothing store called Forward Fashion. They were dressing all the punk stars, people like Richard Simmons—with all that glitter stuff—helping to design this store, planning the lighting, looking at the financial books, and getting them a bookkeeper. So, I did that for about a year.

Anytime I had gotten to that point—that kind of desperate feeling—I've gotten an answer. And then I said, "You know, I love communicating with You, but I can't keep up this kind of emotional intensity. You only talk to us when it gets this bad. If it takes this kind of intensity to contact You, no wonder people don't talk to You!" That real focused intensity is not an easy thing to keep up artificially.

I had sublet an apartment from Holly Woodlawn—a famous transvestite actress—in Greenwich Village on Gay Street. Top floor, garret apartment, big skylights. A fabulous place. It was like a whole 'nother life, going from 3000 square feet, then to a loft, and now to this nice, small, picturesque garret apartment.

But eventually Holly Woodlawn needed to move back into her own apartment, and so I needed to move again. Every couple of years there seemed to be a change.

I was walking around New York City, again. I kept thinking, "I need something more altruistic." When I had been at the gallery, at least I had been helping poor artists. For me to be happy, there has to be a bit of altruistic purpose in any job.

In fall of 1986 was when I heard about this New York Open Center, a place for holistic education. It was just starting. They didn't have any real jobs open, but the thing they did need was a janitor. So I said, "I'll do that." Started at the bottom, minimal salary, but I wanted to be there. The place was altruistic. I *needed* to be there.

I had no permanent address for six years. I took sublets, and stayed with people, and housesat. So, in order for this new job to work, a friend of mine let me move into his loft, and I lived behind the bookcase for two years! Otherwise, I couldn't afford a place, because I had taken an altruistic job with such a low salary.

It was a difficult job, mainly because there was a person there that felt threatened by me.

Can you believe being threatened by a janitor? Well, it's because I know too much. I've finally realized that I was overqualified for this life. I don't have a filter that filters what I think. If I see something, I say it. Not everyone's able to hear that. Oh yes, I can drive people crazy. 95% of the time, what I say is correct, but that doesn't help people's reaction to it. I was more qualified to do this person's job than this person was, so they got threatened. They started telling lies. After I left, they actually came up to me and apologized.

The "one story skyscraper" I built at Temenos, that we called Pine Cabin.

BUILDING CABINS

I was still going to Temenos in Shutesbury, near Amherst, Massachusetts during each summer, building my first cabin there. I was getting donations from friends for building this cabin. It was a big cabin. No electricity. All I had was a chainsaw, a hammer & a hand saw. The cabin was 18 feet by 24 feet, a nice sized cabin. Big window wall, all glass. Skylights. I drew up the plans and took them to the building department. The building official looks at it, and looks at it, and looks at it. And he says, "I've never seen one like this. It's a bit different, but it will work."

And I say to myself, "What does he mean? It seems normal to me." Then I realized I had lived in New York City. I had been watching them build skyscrapers. What I had designed was a one-story skyscraper! I had put the four corners in, and the beams across, and then filled in everything in between. Major undertaking. It took several years. We called this first cabin, "Pine Cabin."

At Temenos, it was even more primitive than Ananda's Meditation Retreat used to be. There was a well to draw water from. At the beginning, we were building a lodge, and we needed an oak post. So, we sat and meditated, and asked this big oak tree if we could take it as a post for this building. And I was sitting there, and I heard this big, stately voice say, "We'd be proud to be a post for that building! Just be respectful of our elders."

Why did I keep going up to Temenos? It was about connection. It was altruistic. It was gentle, and Buddhist, and Quaker. It was Native American sacred ground. It was much the same as what I get here at Ananda's Meditation Retreat. I just felt connected, and adored these people. Temenos is what took my earlier Egypt experience and my India experience, and gave it direction into New Age spirituality, which brought me into this yogic tradition. They would have workshops and people would come up for retreats. They would have weeklong events. We would have Sufis come for Sufi retreats. We would have an Iranian Sufi come and lead a retreat. And so I watched all of this. I didn't take any of these classes. But we meditated three times a day together. I learn by watching. That's the reason I was able to build my cabin like a skyscraper. I watched, and learned.

I made it a requirement of my many jobs in New York City that I could get away during the summers to go work on this cabin. I would spend four, five, or six weeks in the summer. New York is quiet in the summer. No one wanted to stay there then. Actually, I adore New York in August. Everybody's gone. But I wasn't going up to Temenos only in the summers. I would go up all kinds of weekends.

I kept going up to Temenos, with Teresina and her psychologist husband. After three summers of this, I was walking along a path, sort of dejected, and thinking, "How much longer do I have to stay in New York City?" I knew it had been sort of a mandated sentence.

And again, this big voice calls out, "Threeee moooore yeeeears."

I cried out, "What?"

"Threeee mooore yeeeears". I didn't ask any more questions. I just resigned myself to it.

I do hear these voices every once in a while. They're always somewhat comical. Never profound. Often, they sound like they're in an echo chamber, or as if it's coming from a big megaphone. Often, it's when I'm really up against a wall, and just can't figure something out, and I really need some help. It will blast out something like "You fool. It's the chilis!"

MR. KENNETH'S BEAUTY SALON

So, I come home each weekend after working on this cabin, and I'm exhausted. All I wanted to do was sleep. And the person whose bookcase I'm sleeping behind was part of the design team that had just re-designed Mr. Kenneth's Beauty Salon. Five floors of beauty. And he says, "Charles, we need a mirror rehung at Mr. Kenneth's. Could you do that?" Well, I couldn't tell him no, because I'm living rent-free behind his bookcase.

Mr. Kenneth's was the premier beauty salon in the world. He did Jackie Kennedy Onassis's hair. The only hairdresser to ever receive a Cody award, a big design award. So, my entre to the premier beauty salon in the world was that I was asked to hang this mirror. Then, of course, they had other things for me to do, and I did them. So, I get home, and Gerald says, "Oh, Mr. Kenneth called and said he wants you to come work there."

I say, "I'm not gonna go work in some beauty salon! What do ya mean?" I didn't want this job. Apparently, Mr. Kenneth himself had noticed me that day. So, I sort of *had* to go for the interview.

Just before the interview, I had lunch with a couple of people. And one of them, who knew I was going for this interview, said, "You know, my father is an artist. He's a painter. And one time someone said to him, 'How much is that painting?' My father's answer had been, 'It's $2000, or 1500.' The buyer got the 1500. If my father had just said 2000, he would've gotten that." The lesson was clear: you can always come down. So, I thought, "This was a piece of information to remember."

This interview was for what at the time should have been an $18,000 a year job. It was for the Super—the head janitor—and I didn't have to DO anything. I just had to direct it and know what had to be done. But I didn't really want the job. So, I went to the interview grudgingly. And Mr. Kenneth says, "What kind of salary would you want?" Cheekily, I said "$30,000". An impossible amount. I put my answer so high so that of course he'd say no.

And he said, very matter of fact, "OK."

"You know, I need six weeks off in the summer to go to my retreat center, with pay."

And he said, "OK."

"And you know, I also need two weeks in the winter for my mental health." I thought that would surely break the deal.

And he said, "OK." I was just trying to get him to say no, but he never did. So, the job ended up paying $30,000!

So, in late 1987, I got this job, had a staff of 14. And all I'd done was three little fix-it tasks in the store. My job colloquially was known as "the Super", or the fix-it guy. But my official title was "the Qualified Building Engineer," though in actuality I wasn't qualified for it. I didn't know about all this mopping of floors, about the cleaning chemicals and all this janitorial stuff over which I was being put in charge. I had maids. This is where I learned to drink coffee for the first time, because I oversaw the supplies. I had to order all these different kinds of coffee, so I had to learn all about them.

Instead of being qualified as the "Qualified Building Engineer", what I actually did was I listened to the place. Kind of like what I do now at the Meditation Retreat, but now it's with plants!

One thing we had in this five-story building was a steam room, not huge, perhaps 15 feet across. This whole building was run off steam, hot steam from the main power plant in New York City—a big building with smoke coming out of the smokestacks. Every so often the manholes covers in the streets would blow off because of some explosion in the pipe. Nobody in the hair salon would go near this room. It was all these pipes and valves and connections, hot steam coming in off the street. It made horrendous noises. "Clang clang, bing bang." You could almost go deaf in there. Every day I would go in, stand, and just listen. We weren't allowed to touch anything. It could be deadly if something happened. But I would listen. And one day I went in, and instead of "Clang clang bing bang" it went "clang clang chink chug".

So, I called the steam people, and said, "It's making this strange noise." Right away they came out and, boom, they caught it.

Now after this happened at least three times—at this time these guys were $75 an hour, and you had to have two of them just to come out and look at it because it was so dangerous—these guys said, "You know, you've saved this company over $50,000 by calling us early." By me merely listening to this steam stuff!

Another thing we had in this big building was a light bulb room—this big room with all the light bulbs for the place, with all different kinds of bulbs. And I said, "This is sort of silly. We've got all these cases of obsolescent light bulbs." I arranged to have a bunch sent back. I would get little gifts now and then from this company. I got a little TV set, and I'd put it in the kitchen area and organized a drawing: "Who's going to win this?" I didn't want it. I finally came to the realization, "The light bulb company is ripping us off." So, I called around and got some different prices, and found they really *were* ripping us off. So, I fired them.

Their salesman was in the elevator with me carrying all these extra bulbs out of the building, and he was crying because I had cancelled his gift horse. And he says, "How am I going to pay for my house in Florida?"

I said, "Well, you'll figure a way, but not here!"

During this same period, I noticed that the garbage bill was quite high. So, I called the garbage company and asked if they couldn't come and talk to me. I told Mr. Kenneth about it, and he says, "Oh my god, that's the Mafia!"

And their rep shows up and says to me, "Hey, you got a *problem*?" And I talked to him for a while and told him I just thought it was kind of high, especially since we were now creating only half the garbage we used to do. But I was aware this was the Mafia, so we were just chatting. That was all. But nothing ever came from it. The price never came down.

So, it was an interesting job. I had to learn about doing janitorial stuff, because if my night cleaner didn't show up, I had to do it. In this job I also realized a talent I had for putting Charles aside. Mr. Kenneth was a very strong, powerful personality. I just did everything as he would want it done, not as *I* would have wanted it. Interesting. I did this job, like so many others, for two years.

And that gave me enough money to fund a third cabin at Temenos. When I first got there, they only had one cabin for rent. Then I added a second one for them. That cabin that I built at Temenos ended up like a one-story skyscraper. Unconventional to be sure. Somewhat incongruously, we named it "Pine Cabin." But they needed more spaces to help give them income. In addition, what was I going to do up there all summer if I'm not doing *something*? It just seemed appropriate. So now I started a third cabin, my second. But for this cabin, I would go home at night and read the *How to Build a Cabin* book, and the next day do that next step. For about two months, when it was time to finish the interior of the cabin, I lived in it. It was all built out of scrap material, like recycled windows, doors, sinks, stoves. The back of this cabin had a little deck that looked out. We ended up naming this second of the cabins I built "T.knoll," or Teresina's Knoll, in honor of Teresina. I spent many summers up there at Temenos—all the 80's. While I was there it was like seventh heaven.

1990s

LISTENING, AND NOT LISTENING

About this same time, I knew there was change coming. The directors of Temenos were getting old and decided to leave the Retreat to move to the west coast.

Temenos is still operating to this day with a new board of directors, functioning in much the same way that Teresina and Joe had set it up. The cabins there are always rented, just like our cabins at the Meditation Retreat. Teresa and Joe were all about social activism. If I had taken it over, as I could have, I would have inevitably changed it. Although I attended all the marches, I don't have that same kind of passion for social activism that they did.

But then I started getting claustrophobia in those mountains—too many trees. I need to go to someplace more open.

By now I realized I was coming up to the end of "three more years". But I'd been good. I hadn't asked again.

I was giving $5 every day to this homeless man in the subway. I felt very good about that. If I was going on vacation, I would give someone at Mr. Kenneth's a bunch of $5 bills so that he wouldn't miss getting his $5. It was just wonderful. He would see me coming up the steps of the subway, and he would just brighten. It was terrific. And this daily giving, plus Temenos, were my charities. I felt I had to tithe someplace. All that money wasn't for *me*. I had to pay some kind of tax, by sharing it somewhere.

And again, I'm in the subway, just like when I got that most ludicrous thing I could think of—the guidance to "Go around the world." And again, this time, the subway was packed. I say to myself, "You can't ask in here. You've got to find someplace quiet!" But I just say anyway, "Oh, can I go? Can I leave New York now?"

And it was like Tinkerbell flew through the subway car, sprinkling gold dust. The whole car was filled with golden light. And I jumped up, and I shouted, "It's a YES!"

But this was New York. So, no one even noticed!

But soon I start asking myself, "Where're ya gonna go? What're ya gonna do? Where're ya gonna go. What're ya gonna do?" Constant, over and over! It began to drive me crazy. And one day, I went over to Lincoln Center and was sitting by the reflecting pool looking at the sculptures. And this was going on over and over, and finally this voice breaks through, and says, "Charles, you don't have to go anywhere, and you don't have to do anything." Boom! It all stopped.

But suddenly, I *did* know exactly where to go and what to do. This plan popped in: Go to San Diego and help my friend remodel his house. Buy a car and zigzag my way across the Southwest. And see where I might want to land someday. Then go to Florida. And? And? But that's all I got. The guidance stopped there. It didn't really come in words. I just *knew!*

Intuition comes in different ways to different people--some see things, some hear things. I'm in the group that just knows things.

So, in early 1990, I said goodbye to Mr. Kenneth.

And I did everything the guidance said. I went to San Diego. That's where I bought Bwana, my big Land Cruiser.

Before I headed off across the Southwest, my friend Mark was driving me up the coast highway through Encinitas, and he says, "Oh, this is Yogananda's place. You'd like Yogananda." He started to turn in, and white fear came over me. I grabbed the steering wheel and yelled, "NO, NO, NO, NO. Don't go in there!" And instantly I wondered, "Why on earth did I do that? I would have loved to have gone in there." But after making such a fuss, I was too embarrassed. And I was sad because I loved Yogananda. But if I had gone in there *then,* Yogananda would have lost me. Because that would have meant I would have had to find him through SRF[7]. And I definitely would *not* have fit in there.

I spent six weeks zigzagging with Bwana across the Southwest. Then went to Florida—under duress—and stayed with my brother, Rick, and his wife, Carolyn. I had grown up in south Florida, but this time I was to be in central Florida. That area is known as Little Ohio because there are so many Mid-westerners there. The section I grew up in was for people from the Northeast—the people who went to West Palm Beach and the Miami area. The Canadians went to Sarasota and Bradenton, the other side of the state. The whole state is broken up into sections. Where I was now, where my brother lived, were all the born-again Christians. People like me had to stay very quiet. These people could be deadly—persecution territory. No way could I relate to this. I did not like it. It was really uncomfortable for me. I couldn't see how this was going to end well.

My sister-in-law was really upset with me because I kept saying I was going to leave. But I didn't go yet. I haven't moved without getting guidance since 1979. I always wait until I get guidance to do anything now.

Only one time did I do something without guidance. How did it work out? Disaster! I hadn't gotten guidance to do it. All the guidance had said was "go to Florida". The same person, Mark, whom I had helped to remodel a house in San Diego was thinking to remodel another house in Florida to sell. We had such a good relationship. We had become good friends. I had met up with him in Southern California, but now he came out to join me in Florida. We were going to remodel a house and split the profits, which would fund me for a while. I was a little miserable, being stuck in Florida again, but I kept imagining this house we were to remodel: the kind of property it was probably on, the look of it, horses. We found exactly that kind of house. So, we bought it. We started to remodel it. But now my mother got diagnosed with terminal cancer. Not good!

I hadn't gotten guidance to do this house. All it said was "go to Florida". But I was being busy, decided to make some money, and then I could make further plans for what I would do. But my mom is terminal, and I thought, "OK, now I know why I was to come to Florida." I decided I would go down to West Palm Beach and be with her until my brother could get down. But I'm not good being around sick people. I just don't seem to know what to do.

I'd take her to the doctor. She had already been through all these treatments, had already had a cancer operation, and had ended up with a pacemaker, and was going to have to resume chemotherapy. She's 74. And she says, "You know, what do I need to go through all this for? Do I need to be 75 and miserable?" So, she decided to just let go. They gave her three to four months.

Then my brother came, so I'm driving home on the throughway, and suddenly it just opened up, and I felt all the sorrow in the world. I had to pull over. I was incapacitated by all the grief and sorrow. Not just mine, but everywhere's. Because when the filter opened, it just opened everything. I had to work very hard to pull it back in. I had to learn how to filter it so that I would deal with my own grief, but not with the entire world's grief all at the same time. I didn't yet know yoga techniques. Instead, I pulled over and just breathed.

I was living in the world, in my lower chakras, but I was getting guidance in my higher chakras, and the two were out of sync. I needed to fill in the middle chakra. I had put that part of me—the heart—into a heavily insulated box, protecting it. And this event tore my heart open. Even today I don't let it out a lot. I never knew what needed to be said to Teresina ... and to my mother! My mother told my brother one time, "You know, I used to worry about Charles. But you know, he's got it, in a very strange way, but he's got it."

My mother and I had some karmic issues, as I suspect most families do. She was a very strong woman and wasn't one to be dominated. I remember when she visited me in New York City—I would know better today—I said real strongly to her, "I am *not* your husband. You need to start treating me as your *son*. I cannot fulfill all these little husband roles. If you can accept that, fine. If not, you need to go home!"

After that, she sucked it up. She was a Scorpio lady. Nowadays, I could have had a much better relationship with her. It was never *bad*, but it was so separate. I was gay, and you didn't talk about that back then. I remember one time asking if she really wanted to know about my life, and she didn't. If she had, she could have fulfilled a lot of her own dreams. I would have been able to take her more places, and she could have joined me a little bit in my life. I mean, I was hanging out with Edward Albee, and the Broadway people. I was in the high times in New York City, but it was all intertwined with the gay world. Nowadays, I would be able to tell her. But back then? Back then I couldn't have popped her into a gay nightclub.

She always wanted to be a movie star—truly. My grandmother actually caught her and a girlfriend at the train station, boarding the train to go to Hollywood! At one point, I gave her a big coffee table book of great women movie stars, A-Z, with all their glamour shots. When she had only a few months to live and we moved her from West Palm Beach, one of the few possessions she took with her was that book. It was a desire, one that she failed to achieve this time around. I could have given my mother some of that feeling. I could have taken her to the Copa Cabana. I could have dressed up a little more when I took her to the Opera, instead of wearing my jeans. She *wanted* that. I could have taken her dancing!

Back home in Florida, Mom actually *had* friends who were gay. Some of the young people she was very friendly with at Burdine's were gay. But of course, at that time they weren't yet out, even though they weren't hiding it. When I was 8 to 10 years old, we had a gay couple that lived right next door to us, and the neighbors were always giggling about who was the man, and who of the couple was the woman? Mom, leaning on the wall in front of the house, always joined in those gossip sessions. But other than the gossiping, the neighborhood was friendly to this gay couple. They weren't ostracized. My brother told me he knew about me, and even tried to clue mom in about it. But Mom just didn't want to know. It scared her. So, she missed out on those things she would have liked, if only she hadn't been so scared of my gayness. She died in 1990, so this was true even at that late date. My brother and I didn't talk for 20 years during the 60's and 70's. We've gotten close now in our older years, but not when we were younger—even as children—because we were so different. So, we didn't talk about such things until we were more mature.

It's been difficult. Especially when you're young, you don't understand what's going on, so you have to hide it—you have to mask it—basically, you have to live a lie. Otherwise, you're going to get bullied, or picked on, or not promoted. I learned duplicity very early, self-preservation, really. The society doesn't like people who are very different from them. I was a bit artistic, and right brained, and dyslexic, and spiritual, and psychically sensitive, and gay. Any one of those alone might have made one feel they didn't fit. But when you put it all together, it just made me different. You have to hide all that stuff.

Nevertheless, I was amazed that even though I didn't think I fit, I always got pulled in. People were drawn to me, but I learned early on in the spiritual journey not to try to capitalize on that.

In the middle of all this turmoil, my business partner Mark got weird. Being in Florida was driving him crazy, and he went back to California. So, I'm left here with this unfinished house, remodeling it. I had the expertise to redo the house, but he had the money to pay the bills. It had been a joint project, so how do you go on alone?

Unbeknownst to us, about 600 feet away was a piece of property that the power company owned. On it was a Peaker, which is a jet turbine engine to generate electricity. It's called that because it comes on at peak times when they need extra electricity. It's an expensive proposition. Nobody would want to live next to it, because it's like having a jumbo jet parked outside of your doors, revving its engines. The windows would rattle. This house was known amongst the local realtors as "The Gold Mine". We had bought it for $100,000. We had put about $40,000 into it. It should have sold for $400,000 because it was on one of the most picturesque pieces of property—live oaks with the moss, five acres grandfathered in for horses, five minutes from the throughway. But it had been mothballed for 25 years, so no one remembered the problems it had. Suddenly it turned into something other than a goldmine. I couldn't stay there because all the vibration was making me sick.

I got ahold of the phone number of the president of Florida Power and Light, and immediately he challenges me, "How did you get this number?"

I just said, "I got it." And I continued, "If this were your house, you'd be upset, too." So they sent a team out to monitor the noise, and I went out to talk to the monitors. But they told me there was no correcting this, because it was some kind of low frequency that they really couldn't dampen down. From that point on they were forbidden to talk to me. My friend Mark came back, and we went to see a lawyer, and he explained it. Florida Power and Light is the most powerful corporation in all of Florida. They have all the state senators in their pocket. So, after doing all that work, the best we could do was to sell it back to them for $9000 less than we paid for it.

It was a hundred-year-old house and solid as a rock. It was fabulous. It had an old slave's quarter on it. So, I told another friend, "We're leaving this, and you ought to go in there and salvage what you can." Otherwise, it was going to be torn down. He went in and salvaged what he could. He made $15,000. The doors in there were all handmade, hand-planed doors, $500-600 a piece at that time. My bedroom upstairs was 18 feet square with a big fireplace.

I should have known better because none of this project had come from intuition. It had all been conjured from my imagination. The whole escapade came about because of mere human desire.

So, I had to sell everything I had collected, packed whatever I could take in my truck, Bwana, and drove away, without even looking back at the house. I felt so bad. That house had had a spirit, and I had just killed it.

Now I headed to Temenos, to finish the interior of that second cabin I'd been working on, the one we called "T'knoll", for Teresina's Knoll.

With my brother Rick and his wife Carolyn in Florida, 1983

My mom Emma in her later years

The second cabin I built at Temenos, called T'Knoll

Interior of T'knoll cabin

Before I left Temenos for good, though, they were getting ready to do some forestry work there. They'd marked a bunch of trees for removal. I wasn't there much of the time, and the original founders had already moved to Oregon. I was just there long enough to finish up that second cabin. The grounds man came to me almost in tears, saying, "You know, the forest doesn't want to be cut now. We need to re-think this. *Some* is OK, but a lot is *not!*" He went to the Retreat council—all very aware people that even buy in to the Findhorn principles—and he told them his story, but they ignored him. And now he comes to me, and he says, "The forest really doesn't want this."

So, I tell him, "You disempowered the entire council because you heard something that they didn't. But here's what you do. You need to go home tonight and think of as many reasons as you can why it shouldn't be cut. And then come back and present *that* to them."

He did all that, and they agreed. They could agree with the left-brain stuff, but if someone else had a right-brain experience, they couldn't agree. Not unless they had that experience themselves. Swami would often repeat the advice that just because you get an intuition, doesn't mean that you can use that to convince anybody else. Sweet reason will be much more respected. Even though you *know* what the answer is, you can't use that as a reason that something must be done.

On the other hand, what with my dyslexia, words have never been overly important to me. Consequentially, I get in trouble now and then. I'm not interested in understanding things on a word level. When I hear a philosophical lecture, I create color out of it in my mind, and that has to be re-translated back into words later. The words are not completely accurate, because they are describing something that is already 2 or 3 generations away from the original impetus, something that already was impossible to describe. Today going through all these memories, I am listening to the words, but I'm also translating all those words into pictures, colors, feelings, geometry—the things that work more for me.

So, I finished the interior of that "T.knoll" cabin at Temenos, then drove west. I knew *that* was where I was supposed to go.

BUCKAROO

So, once I got out West, I went to visit Teresina and her husband up in Portland. But I knew I couldn't live up there because it was just too wet and rainy. When I was packing up to leave, someone asked me, "Where are you moving to?" I started to say the Southwest. That's what I was drawn to—I loved the red rock areas. But as soon as I started to say the Southwest, this little light bulb goes on in my head, and I hear this little high whisper, "Oregon." That's not what I had wanted to say, but I go, "You know, I guess I'm going to Oregon." I had learned not to argue with these things. When I had tried to direct life in Florida on my own, look what a disaster I had created.

So, I took the Oregon map, and I found a place way up in the northeast corner called Enterprise. My house in Florida had been in a town called Enterprise. I thought, "I'll go there." So, I start zigzagging my way across Idaho on Forest Service dirt roads on the way to Enterprise, Oregon. There weren't any direct roads up there in those days. Just as I'm about to cross the border, I see these people in bathing suits, even though it was cold. This was in the middle of a high plateau. There was a rock ledge with this maybe 25-foot-long waterfall coming across it, dropping only about 10 feet, and I say, "That's a hot spring!" So, I pulled off, and I took a ritual shower. As you moved along this ledge underneath this water, you had different temperatures. It was fabulous. Gorgeous country. That's where they filmed the Marlboro ads. Gas was like $8 a gallon there in the boonies. And my truck drank it like water.

I found a little place to stay in Enterprise. For dinner, I stopped in this tiny coffee shop, like a diner. And I ask, "Is there any place to rent a horse?" I wanted to ride and see what's going on. Besides, it was too expensive to drive everywhere. So, I thought I'd have an experience on a horse. After all, the Marlboro man did it, why couldn't I? I'd been on a horse some. I used to ride in Central Park occasionally. No formal training, I would just do it.

But the gal behind the counter says, "Oh no, no place around here rents horses.

Then a gal two stools down says, "Oh, Sally's looking for a buckaroo to help bring in the cows." I wasn't sure what the word buckaroo meant, but I knew I wanted to get that job, whatever it was. Turns out "buckaroo" is the name people in Oregon use for a cowboy. And I figure that's almost like renting a horse. The gal on the stool says, "I'll give you the address." Then I talked to her for a while. Turns out she's an artist who knew my gallery in New York. So, she gave me a place to stay for three days while she showed me the sites. Then she gave me a note to take to Sally, who lived on a 3000-acre ranch—which if you flattened out all its mountain peaks would have turned into a 30,000-acre ranch. She lived in a log house with her two children, off the grid, no electricity, a vegetarian. It was a family ranch that she was caretaking. She just rented the pastures out and let the cows graze. Her only obligation was simply to get them all into one pasture so the cowboys could come and pick them up.

So, Sally and I got on horseback, and rounded up 350 cows. But I, of course, didn't know how to round up cows. I'm on this horse, and the *horse* knew how. So, I'm communicating with this horse. I just paid attention, and it taught me how to herd cows. I just followed the horse. It knew exactly what to do.

Its name was Wheezer because it had some lung thing. I was told not to run it hard. Wheezer was a big horse. We had a wonderful time. You have to make a noise when you're herding cows, to let the cows know that you're there. I had to make up something. I'm thinking "yippee-oh kiyay" or some such thing. Kept trying to remember what noises they made in the old cowboy movies. Finally, I came up with "Yip. Yip." That worked.

You herd cows indirectly. I saw a book about this after I had done this. It's all about line of sight. When I saw what this book said, finally I knew what the horse had been trying to teach me.

So we've got these 350 cows and their calves. We got them into this one pasture. But there was one cow and calf left. We would get them going, and then they would take off straight up the side of a mountain. Our horses couldn't go the same way they had. It took us an hour to zigzag around to get up where we could drive them down, and kazoom, they would take off again. After two days of this, the cow and her calf took off across the meadow, and Wheezer and I communicated to each other by simultaneously thinking, "Enough!" We took off across this meadow running flat out. But halfway across the meadow I became "un-one" with the horse. I was not touching the saddle. The only thing holding me was I had hold of the reins. My feet were out of the stirrups. I'd bounce once in a while. We were going, well, I don't know how fast. That horse was after those cows. If I had fallen, I would have killed myself. The horse adjusted a little bit, I came back down and settled myself. And we got them! The horse, with me flying off, we got those two cows! And Sally comes riding up. She had a friend with her. She was a little bit upset because I had let the horse run hard. But I defended myself, exclaiming, "There was *no* way I could stop her! The horse really wanted to get that job done. Listen to her, she isn't even wheezing." That horse was so happy to have succeeded.

After my first two hours on the horse, I said to myself, "If I were paying for this, I would want to go home now." I had a blister across my whole tailbone area. But five days later, I was still on this horse. I was stuffing T-shirts down there, anything I could find. That darn saddle was the hardest thing I'd ever experienced. Finally, I knew there was one more part of the round-up that was supposed to be done, but I said, "Sally, I think I'm done. I need to get into a hot spring."

When we brought those last two cows up, the cowboys were there getting ready to load all the cattle on the trucks to take them someplace else. They looked up, took one look at me, and started rolling on the ground with laughter. I had on a big poufy down jacket, I had on a cross body murse, adidas tennis shoes, and a baseball cap. Didn't exactly look the part of a rough and tough cowboy. They were just in hysterics. So, I climb down and take their picture. But I *was* a cowboy for a week.

It was like Lahiri's Golden Palace, the one in the *Autobiography of a Yogi* when Lahiri re-took kriya initiation from Babaji. Afterwards, Lahiri laid down next to the river in samadhi for days that he was unable to count. For me, being a cowboy felt like a whole lifetime passing in one week. I slept on Sally's sofa. We had breakfast before sunup. Went out to get the horses. We came back after sunset. Every day I would give her children $5 as they went off to school, because there was a health food store near their school where they would buy me granola bars. I practically lived on granola bars for a week.

BUCKHORN SPRINGS

From Sally's place, I zigzagged through Oregon. I had no idea where I was going. I knew I would know where to stop when I saw it. I drove through Oregon in Bwana, zigzagging my way. I was on my way down to San Francisco. There, I was supposed to visit my friend from India, Jan. My last stop in Oregon, before heading south to San Francisco, ended up being in Ashland. I was driving through the Rogue River Valley, and I look up and here's this table mesa. And over there was Mt. McGlaughlin—just like Mt Fuji. And below that was a desert. It was just like the Southwest. I always thought that I was eventually going to end up in the Southwest. And I drive down into Ashland, drove through town—a cute little town—and ended up parking right in front of the old co-op. I said, "Oh, they've got a co-op!" And I walk inside into the middle of that store. And I breathe in deep, and say, "This smells like home."

I did visit my friends in San Francisco, but Jan and her family were thinking of moving out of San Francisco. So, she and her husband followed me back up to Ashland. We took a Bed and Breakfast together for about a week. We explored, looking for houses, but couldn't find anything to buy. She says, "You know, I have the reference for a friend of a friend." So, she looked him up.

It was a gay couple, two guys. Just everything clicked. They were leaving in three days to go on a two- or three-week trip somewhere. One of them handed me the keys to their house. The other one later said, "You know, he doesn't even let people stay overnight." He must have been an old friend from past lives. So, I stayed for three weeks. One of their mothers had bought a condominium in Ashland but wasn't staying there. She lived in Pasadena.

Entrance sign to Buckhorn Springs

So, I asked, "Would she let me stay there? I could afford only this much rent," which was way below what it should have been. So they called her. She said yes, so I settled in Ashland in the fall of 1990, and I lived there for four or five months through the winter.

I kept looking out my view from the condo to the East, up into those mountains. I was yearning to go up there. And someone told me about a place called Buckhorn. One day I'm driving up in those mountains, and I see this sign for Buckhorn Springs Road.

It was a dirt road, but I turned and went in. There was this little 100-year-old Inn that they were remodeling. I talked to them for a while. They said they were going to be finished in the spring.

I knew I didn't want to be there during the winter. Heck, they were already wearing heavy coats, and breathing out steam vapor. I was no fool. When spring of 1991 came, I called them to see if there was any work. But they said, "No, there isn't any."

"Well, then can I volunteer you a day? You must have something that needs to be done that you can't get to." They were blown away that anyone would do that. So I went, and they had me outside raking the yard area. After about two hours this was killing me. I hadn't done physical work in months.

But the guy comes out and says, "I don't know if you would want this or not, but our laborer didn't show up to help the guy who's plastering. Would you be interested?"

And I said, "Oh sure." So here I am mixing plaster and hauling the stuff up and down stairs. When I finally went home, I was dead-tired. Just dead. But over time, I became indispensable to them.

And I had to move out of my other place, and so in the spring of 1991, I moved into a nice cozy trailer there at Buckhorn. My trailer there I called "Peachy." Admittedly, it is a bit of a comedown when you move into a trailer after having lived in a 3000 square foot house in Manhattan.

The first winter, it got too cold in the trailer, so I went to Mexico and Guatemala, and spent the winter there. I think of each year as going from September to September, like a school year, rather than a calendar year. That's how I place things chronologically in my mind. And I'm dyslexic. So, 1992 in my mind is really Sept 1991-Sept 1992.

I arrived at Buckhorn just before it was opened to the public in the spring of 1991. We were still putting the doorknobs on as the first guests were arriving for a wedding. The owner Leslie Sargent wrote in her book about Buckhorn: "Everywhere that Charles went, terraced gardens, bright paint, and invaluable advice followed. He became the gardener, designer, concierge, waiter, breakfast cook, resident, and everyone's counselor." I loved working for that woman.

I stayed there at Buckhorn the first time, just like with many of my jobs previously, for two years.

Cooking for the guests at Buckhorn Springs

Guest cabins at Buckhorn

Near the end of my first stint at Buckhorn, while I was relaxing off-duty in my trailer one evening, I get a call from the dining room. I hear this plaintive voice over the phone, "We have people from New York here, and the waitress is in tears!" So, I got dressed really quick and zoomed down. And I go to this table. It's got about twelve or fourteen people. I rapped authoritatively on the tabletop, and call out, "Attention! Attention! I'm only going to do this once. This is the menu. These are your choices. Now pay attention." I went through it all. And they shut up. We got through the whole meal. The bill was hundreds of dollars. And they were leaving. There was this big pile of cash, and I counted it. But there was only a $5 tip. And I call out, "Hold it! This is a four-hundred-dollar tab, and you've left me $5 to put up with all this nonsense? More!"

So anytime anybody from New York City came, the restaurant staff always made sure that I was going to be on duty. For abruptness, New York people trump L.A. people any day.

Buckhorn seemed like Paradise to me: Native American sacred ground, and working with wonderful, good co-workers. But after a couple of years, I felt unsettled. I thought, "Well, you're living in Paradise. This is just exactly what you would pick on your own. So, what's wrong?" And I thought, "Well, I don't have a good enough purpose." It wasn't an altruistic place. It was a commercial thing, a privately owned place for making money. Sure, it put food in my mouth and a roof over my head. We had groups coming in and doing things. But by about two-thirds through my second year at Buckhorn Springs, it just didn't seem enough.

So, one day I go onto my little private deck off the trailer, and I look out. Through the bushes, I had cut out a view of Pilot Rock. And I looked out at this rock, and for the next month, twice a day, I just screamed, "I don't know what to do. I know so many ways to pray, but I don't know which one to use. I know so many ways to *meditate*, but I don't know which one to use. I'm doing nothing—*nothing,* do you hear me? —until you send me a teacher. That's *it!*"

DEVI

It must have been heard. Because about a month and a half later, I'm down in the main kitchen, and they said, "Oh, we have a group of ministers coming in a couple of weeks." And I think, "What kind of ministers? Some of these people can be dangerous. We need to figure out how to modify our behavior." So, I say, "We better ask them ahead of time for a packet of material."

Soon after, the packet came, and it was sitting on the counter, but nobody else seemed interested, so I picked it up and took it to my room to read it. I got home, took out my chair, opened the packet up, and the first thing I saw was a picture of Yogananda. I just started to cry, because now I *knew* why these people were coming.

Once they all arrived, I watched them like a hawk. I was too bashful to say anything to anybody, and I couldn't tell who the leader of this group was. The people at the lodge had told me, "Oh, they might bring their Swami." And I said, "Oh, I hope not."

Going back in time a bit ... when I worked at the New York Open Center, I had helped them build their bookstore. I'd designed all the shelves and everything. And as we're putting out all these books onto the shelf, I cry out, "Who ordered this despicable book?" It was Swami Kriyananda from Ananda Village doing the yoga postures! I had a very strong past life reaction, without even knowing who he was. As it turned out, if he had come with the group to Buckhorn, I know I never would have come to Ananda Village.

But luckily, I met all his lieutenants instead. I didn't know that *he* was the one in charge of this whole group, because the packet they had sent to Buckhorn only showed Yogananda's picture.

So, I served all these ministers' breakfast in the lodge, and then I went to check their rooms, to see if they need towels or anything. My usual practice would be to knock first, and call out, "Housekeeping." But I was certain the whole Ananda group was in the breakfast room, so this time I didn't, and I went in unannounced. The washbasin was in the bedroom proper, and the rest of the bathroom was behind doors. So, I see they need towels, and I went back out to get clean towels from the cart. But as I re-entered the room, I ran into this little woman.

And I called out, "Can I help you?" And I think, "That's a strange thing to say, Charles, instead of 'excuse me', or 'pardon me.'"

But then I saw there was a tear in her eye, and she says gently, "Yes, I've just dropped a very sentimental pearl earring down the sink." What I didn't know is that she had just prayed, "Master, I need some help."

And that's the very moment I had popped in and called out, "Can I help you?"

I went over, assessed what had happened, and tried to lower her expectations by stating, "This is all mineral water, so the pipes are all encrusted." Nevertheless, the pipe came right off in my bare hands. I pulled her earring out, wiped it off—I'm still completely embarrassed—and I hand her the precious pearl earring.

I was watching this group constantly. There was this palm tree at one end of an L-shaped room inside the lodge, and they were meeting at the other end of the L. I was hiding behind this palm tree, peeking through the palm leaves. It was like the old *Laugh-In* TV show. I'm peeking through the palm tree, watching them. I still couldn't figure out who their leader was—everybody seemed equal. I'm shy around new people. It's hard to believe, I know, but it's true. So, I didn't talk to anybody, except this one woman whom I had bumped into. When I was setting the table, I would be leaning to the side, with one ear very open, listening in to everything they were saying. Yogananda's former chauffeur, Peggy Dietz, had also attended this gathering, so that way I ended up hearing all of Peggy's stories about the times she was with Master.

It soon got to be their last day at Buckhorn. All these people were down in the lobby with their luggage. And I'm in a panic! I somehow felt I was supposed to go with these people, but I was in a total panic, because I still hadn't *talked* to anybody.

And that same little woman came up to me and whispered, "Why don't you come to Ananda? "

And I whispered back, "OK." I thought, I wanted to talk to the head of this group, but here all I got was what I took to be this mousey little woman. And she says, "Call this number and tell them Devi told you to call. " And I whispered back again, "OK."

Nayaswami Devi

With Uma McFarlane at my very first Shivaratri celebration, 1993

Magi Weber with new merchandise in the Expanding Light Boutique

ANANDA VILLAGE

So, I finished up at Buckhorn, and two weeks later, in December of 1992, I was at Ananda Village, outside Nevada City, California. Devi Novak, together with her husband Jyotish, are the Spiritual Directors of all of Ananda Worldwide. She returned home ahead of me, and she talked about how she had "found this guy" up in Ashland. By the time I arrived, it was like I was already famous. Devi and I obviously had a special past life connection. She just knew I belonged at Ananda.

Devi gave the first Sunday Service after I arrived at Ananda. I sat there, and I was entranced. But I wasn't seeing Devi. Instead, I saw a full-fledged general up there, pacing back and forth, inspiring the troops, in full uniform—like I was seeing her in a past life. So, as she was leaving after the service, I say to her, "Hey, do you think you've ever been a general in a past life?" Slowly, with a little smile, she said "Yes." It's obvious to me that she and I go way back together.

I knew I was right to be at Ananda. That first Sunday Service I sat near the back and looked across the back of people's heads. When I see a person that I know from past lives, I get a little electric buzz in my root chakra. I had not made new friends or even talked very much with people for years, because I wasn't going to waste time with people I didn't already know—from past lives, I mean. I could have an acquaintance with someone, but not more than that unless there was that past life connection. So, when I looked across the backs of those heads in the Expanding Light temple, and I felt that little electrical "zt, zt, zt"—that's how I know I'm witnessing a past life connection—I just knew. I've learned to recognize it.

In December, January, and February, of '92-'93, I was with Haridas Blake (who, until recently ran Ananda's teaching center with his wife Roma in Bangalore, India) for Work Exchange at the Expanding Light—Ananda's retreat outside Nevada City, CA. Then I was with Uma McFarlane (who teaches now at Ananda's colony in Assisi, Italy) for a weeklong course in Discipleship. It got to the day before our Discipleship Ceremony, and I had been nervous about taking those vows. Those were not light steps for me. Discipleship, you know, that's a sacred thing. One doesn't mess around with that stuff. Uma said, "Oh, Charles, just do it!" I was at the morning meditation, daydreaming rather than meditating, and I look at the clock and say to myself, "Ya know, I've only got a few minutes left, I better start meditating. And tomorrow I'm gonna be a disciple of Yogananda." And from somewhere I heard, "How about *now*?" Instantly I went into bliss. I had a flashback. It was like those life reviews that happen when people die. I saw every place in this lifetime that Master had touched or nudged me, and where he had guided my life ever since I read *Autobiography of a Yogi*, which was back in 1978. That's what had sent me to India. Master had sent me there, I saw now. It was clear that all that had happened had brought me to this very point. I could only handle this feeling for short times. One can't afford to hang out in bliss for too long if you're expected to do Work Exchange.

We went as a group with Uma to the Crystal Hermitage—Swami's former residence at Ananda Village—to meditate. Halfway through the meditation, I just threw my hand over my mouth. I was ready to break into hysterical laughter. But there was enough of "me" still present, who said, "You can't do that *here*!"

So, I went outside, and the belly laughs spilled out. Suddenly, I understood that song, "Some of us laugh, Mother, some of us weep, and some of us dance with Thy sweet joy!"

I knew that one of the reasons I was at Ananda was to get initiation into Kriya Yoga. But at the Village in those days, it usually took a very long time of preparation to get Kriya. I'd been here only December, January, February, and March. Now it was time for the next Living Discipleship program to start, and Dhyana Smith (now co-Spiritual Director of Ananda India) was meeting with different people about Kriya Yoga—Yogananda's premier meditation technique. I said, "No, I didn't have kriya yet, but I would like to get it." Dhyana looked deeply at me—penetratingly—and announced firmly, "You're ready!" I thought, "But I need more time!" She went right inside. She said, "No, you're ready." And boom, boom, boom, I had kriya. I hear that's how Master used to do it. It had been a matter of whether this person had the right consciousness so that kriya could help them.

MEDITATION RETREAT

I arrived at the Meditation Retreat for the first time in March of 1993. By that time, I had used up most of my money. So, my first three months at the Retreat I was on work exchange. I was among the earliest workers ever on work exchange up at the Meditation Retreat. David and Karen (now Anaya) Gamow (who serve at Ananda Palo Alto now) were the on-site managers for the Retreat back then, under the ministerial guidance of Anandi and Bharat Cornell (some of Ananda's best-known teachers and writers.)

David and Karen had recently finished rebuilding the Meditation Retreat's temple. David tells an amazing backstory about this: "Vidura Smallen (who for the last decade has been running this Retreat with his wife Durga) asked us to manage the Retreat one afternoon in February 1992. *That very night* the temple collapsed. I called the next morning saying, 'You know... if you want to take that as a sign from Master, I won't hold it against you if you renege on your job offer.' He said, 'Are you kidding? Your job has now expanded to include building a new temple!'"

Dambara Begley (who recently finished working a year at The Expanding Light guest services) always chose the same favorite spot where he sat for meditation. He had been all alone in the temple that evening. Then suddenly a thought came into Dambara's head to move. Whether this was because he recognized it as guidance, or just because he was cold, in any case he got up and uncharacteristically moved way back along the left side wall near the propane heater. Having moved the Temple's harmonium back with him, he started chanting Yogananda's "They Have Heard Thy Name." Suddenly, in the middle of that chant, almost the entire roof of the temple came avalanching down toward him. The only exception was one small piece over him, which remained held up only due to the two exit door frames. The roof came down with such force that an upright piano against the temple wall had been flipped over on its back. The front two-thirds of the temple was completely gone, having collapsed right up to, and including just on top of, the harmonium he had been playing. Stunned, he realized that if he hadn't moved back when he did, he himself would have been crushed.

We are taught in beginning meditation classes not to pay attention to our thoughts during meditation. However, Dambara recognized this one as true guidance. Lucky for him!

My first assignment on work exchange was to help Rodrick Anderson (a disciple and carpenter formerly from New Zealand) fix the old office dome. The old common dome, where both the kitchen and the dining room had been previously, was still standing, and the newly re-built temple had just been finished. It was raining and there was lots of sticky red clay. We were walking on wooden planks to get into the temple, but nevertheless our clothes were red, the dining room floor turned red, even our hair got streaks of red. It was a mess all around.

Dambara in the old temple

The new Temple of Silence at Meditation Retreat, my first landscaping job at Ananda.

Rhododendrons

Then David and Karen heard that I had a little bit of landscaping background, so they asked if I would landscape the new temple. But I wanted to be inward and quiet, and one must be very careful, because creativity can fan the ego. It makes it very difficult to discern which is which—is it ego, or is it true guidance? So, I kept answering "No."

But in that spring of 1993, I came out of the temple one day and called out, "Who drew all those lines on the ground?" Like somebody had taken chalk and drawn lines. And the person next to me said, "What lines, Charles?" And I said, "Uh oh!" I knew immediately that it was something I was going to have to do. These lines were a simple landscaping plan, and all I would have to do would be to follow the lines. I don't tell people this to build myself up. I only supplied the muscle. I could never have figured all this out on my *own*. So, I went back to Karen and David and said, "OK, I'll do it.

Therefore, it was only because of this guidance that I agreed to landscape around the temple. But back then we didn't have enough water, so we couldn't put in any plants. And I kept envisioning the temple being in a lake. So, I convinced the Gamows that we could buy river rock—I figured at least it's water rock—and we could make it look like a *dry* lake. So, we put all the rock walls and boulders and things around the temple. And that was it. Two successive groups of Living Discipleship students (the program we called Monastic Training back then) helped us finish the job. During 1993 that's all we could do.

It was a minor miracle that David Gamow even approved the purchase of all the big rocks for this project. Ananda was in a financial crunch right then. You could tell, because the leaders were always walking around with such serious expressions—like we were so far in the red. At one point, some months later, I saw our boss Gyandev McCord (who now heads up Ananda's Yoga Teacher Training), and I commented, "Oh, you're *smiling!*"

And he said, "Yes, because we're in the *black!*" I didn't realize how much this had weighed on David at the time, but I knew it must have. We were pinching pennies everywhere. So, to spend $5000 on big rocks seemed ridiculous. And David Gamow is, of course, best known as a finance and money guy. It's just one of the signs that it had to have been divinely guided—he approved this project with absolutely no assurances. He didn't really know who I was. Karen and I are connected, and she knew my work over at the Expanding Light. I suspect she engineered my coming up to the Meditation Retreat in the first place. I didn't even have to beg for the money. It's true that it wasn't $5000 all at once. We'd get this load and get this much done. Then I'd say to David, "I could do *this* much more if we had another load." "Do it," he'd answer. And it happened time and again! I mean, it's so much *not* like him to never question what I needed each next load for, nor even how much it was going to cost!

In those days, the entire "top" of the mountain at the Retreat was solid manzanita. You couldn't see one building from another. It was just manzanita scrub with these little paths through it. If you got off the path, you were in trouble. When it was just raw manzanita and oak and pine forest up here, people didn't tend to linger. They came and took care of their business, then left. It was a very harsh environment. It was very, very yang.

The lines I was seeing suggested one path that went off through the manzanita to nowhere. And I was laying it out in little stones, and I stood back and looked at it and I said, "This is ridiculous. The widest path up here is thirty-six inches, and this path doesn't even go anywhere, and yet it's six feet wide. That's just silly!" So, I started pulling the rocks back in to outline a path three feet across.

You know how when a car with a huge bass speaker comes up behind you, "Boom, boom, boom," and you can feel it even more than hear it. And I heard, "I said SIX feet! This is going to be a place of PILGRIMAGE." I think I went icy cold. I must have turned pale. I immediately started moving the rocks back to six feet, saying, "OK, I'm puttin' 'em back! See, I'm puttin' 'em back!"

I knew then that I was dealing with a high spirit. Now that happened thirty years ago when we didn't know all that was going to occur up here. That path didn't go anywhere until the dining room building was built in 2001. And now it's a main path at the Retreat. It's the one that goes by Mother's Pond. Something was guiding all this, and it's all tied together.

Even though it went nowhere, we graveled that path and everything. Meridian from the Ananda Berkeley Meditation Group was here on Living Discipleship, and we had about ten minutes before the end of the work shift. She came up to me—she was just covered in sweat, dust, and dirt, and fairly exhausted—and she said, "Can I go? I need to go take a shower. "

When I heard, "I said six feet!", I instantly made the path wider.

I said, "Darling, I need this pile of rock. This is your last day, and I need this pile of rock moved." They were good–sized rocks, too. I said, "Just take and pick them up and hold them to your stomach. Walk slowly. And imagine yourself pregnant with Divine Mother." So, she did. I walked over and saw that she really got *into* it. It was just a meditative state. It became time to go—she still hadn't finished the pile, and I said, "OK, we can go now." And she said, "No". She stayed until she finished that pile. I saw her ten years later, and that very task had become for her the high point of her time with us. She had really connected, and went very deep, beyond her normal self.

HEALTH FOOD STORES, HERE AND THERE

In June of 1993 I entered what's nowadays called the Living Discipleship program—it was known back then as Monastic Training—headed up that year by Anandi and Bharat. The last week of the program they had us volunteer in different departments around the community, and they signed me up for a day at the Earth Song store that back then Ananda ran in Nevada City. They assigned me to the restaurant half of the store. I was in a near panic—shades of my old burn-out at the UN Plaza Hotel in New York City. It brought up all those old memories. But I put all that aside, and I just worked that whole day. On the way out the door, Ivor Sowton said to me, "How did you do?"

I said, "I don't know, I just worked." I went and got into my car, and I just sat there, catatonic, almost shaking, because it brought all that stuff up from the past. It was at least twenty minutes before I could even turn the key. To drive home I couldn't go any more than twenty-five or thirty miles per hours. And I'm praying, "Please, please, please! If they assign me long-term to Earthsong, please give me the strength to do it. I'm here to serve, and I need to be able to do this. Please, please help!" It was constant, deep soul prayers. Then that night I had a dream, a very vivid dream. I was in the *grocery* store side of Earthsong. I was putting stuff up on the shelf, and I was in bliss. And I thought, "Oh, thank you." So that's exactly where I ended up, in the grocery side rather than the restaurant side of the store. I made it my goal while working at Earthsong to see God in each jar of spaghetti sauce. And I achieved it!

The bulk food guy at Ananda's Earthsong store, both the old and the new, in Nevada City.

So, after I'd been at the Meditation Retreat the first time for seven-eight months, I moved to the Village and worked at Earth Song. I ended up helping the transition from the old Earthsong to the new Earthsong, which Ananda later sold, and it became California Organics Market in Nevada City, CA. I was at Earthsong for four years. It was one of the favorite jobs I ever had. I did the bulk food section, then I did all the ordering for the rest of the store. This was my first real job after taking the Living Discipleship program, beginning in summer 1993 until I went back to Ashland in 1997.

About 1996, Nakula Cryer had finished rebuilding the Lahiri Mandir at The Expanding Light. They were looking for someone to landscape it. But I already had a full-time job at Earthsong. One Sunday for Sunday Service I parked up above the amphitheater, which I just don't do, because you must walk back uphill to retrieve your car. That's not something that's easy for me with my "polioed" diaphragm. But I was late this day, and I zoomed down from that upper parking lot. And on the way back, I was walking toward the upper parking lot past the Lahiri Mandir, and as I turned to the left, I saw a vortex swirling around the mandir. I knew this was a sign. I just said, "Uh-oh. You've got to figure out how you're gonna do this," since I had the other job already. But I told them, "OK, I'll do it."

This vortex went out, in a counterclockwise direction. I didn't know all this at the time—vortex as a term probably didn't pop into my head, but even then, I recognized it as something turning. I just saw the whirlpool of energy, and the size. This is what I mean about words. I have to go back into that experience and paste words onto it. The experience didn't come with words.

So, I went every morning at 8 a.m., before my work would begin as the night manager at Earthsong. I worked from 8 until 12 at the mandir. Then I ran home, took a shower, and drove to work in Nevada City.

Biraj and I worked on the Lahiri Mandir together during 1996. I left for Ashland soon after that. I was comfortable about leaving the Lahiri Mandir because Biraj had taken it under his wing, with the help of his Expanding Light work exchange students, to see that it continued to get watered. We had already put in an automatic watering system. Biraj kept troubleshooting it. Soon after he left the Expanding Light in 1999, though, a pipe broke, and it never got fixed. So, half of the landscaping died. But the backbone of that landscaping still looks nice. Biraj and I also did the work to landscape The

Expanding Light's Serenity guest house, but we did that one in more of *his* linear way, rather than my more intuitive way.

I have never totally fit at Ananda Village. I've always done things in my own way. Yet while at Ananda, I pledged 100% of my energy to Ananda and its endeavors. My first year at Ananda I always thought I would stay for a few weeks—or maybe a month at most—and then head off to the Southwest. I was still mentally aiming for the Southwest. And many, many years later—more than 30 years to date—here I am still. It was sort of a surprise that it was Devi Novak herself, the Spiritual Director of all of Ananda Worldwide, who got me moving back to Ashland again.

While I was working in the store at Earth Song, Devi would come through my cash register line—it had been *more* than two years, and I was getting really antsy. I always thought I was coming to Ananda simply to pick up some teachings and then I would go and get on with my life. But she said, "No, you're supposed to stay." Inwardly I remember whining, "But they're Hindus? ... How am I supposed to deal with *Hindus?*" I think I must have known Yogananda when he was Buddha. I had always been looking for the Buddhists.

So, the next time she came through my line, I'd said "Devi, Ya know, I'm thinkin' of movin' to Boulder, Colorado." That's where lots of Buddhists were. I'd be checking her groceries out. Devi would put her head down. I would see her thinking. Then she would look up and gently shake her head side to side. She wouldn't say anything, just shook her head, "No." I was continually trying to get away.

Then one day she came through my line again, and I say, "Devi, how about Ashland?" She thought about it briefly, then quietly responded, "Yes!" I made one call, and everything just went blippity blip. I found a place to stay. I had a good job at a very good health food store. Everything just flowed—that's one way you know guidance is right. Devi just approved my own intuition! I won't make a move like that now without Devi's OK.

So, in summer of 1997, after spending over four years at Ananda Village, I moved north to Ashland, Oregon, for the *second* time, and was away from Ananda for four more years before I got back.

It was a very special time in Ashland. I was living at Buckhorn Springs while commuting to Ashland for work. To earn rent at Buckhorn, I did substitute cooking shifts during the week & would wait tables on the weekends. Though I started out in the same old trailer I'd been in previously, next Bruce Sargent restored the top of the old barn into a lovely living space for me. Buckhorn was always under construction! Bruce (who with his wife, Leslie, owned the place) worked on those buildings constantly for several years. On the insides of each building, he followed the building methods and materials exactly like the old-timers had done their work a century before. There were eight rooms in the Buckhorn lodge, plus six cabins, and all together their retreat could probably hold 25 guests.

The board on which the Buckhorn sign is mounted, I found in Tyler Foote Road's Shady Creek, behind Bhavani Girard's house. It was 5 feet across, one piece cut out of an old pine or cedar tree, probably 100 years old. It must have been part of a really big tree. And it was waterlogged, so it took 4 people to pull it out of the creek.

During this second stay in Ashland, Anandi Gray and I hosted a workshop every Wednesday night. The workshop centered on Paramhansa Yogananda's book, *Man's Eternal Quest*. We had 12 people participating—never fewer than nine. Like an encounter group, everyone helped everyone else. The two of us would give an introduction, and then different people would give their impression of what they'd learned from that chapter and how it had touched their life. I don't read easily, but as co-sponsor, I had to concentrate deeply to come up with one or two things to emphasize each week.

I know why I got sent back to Ashland for those years, it was to get me away from the Village during the lawsuit Ananda was going through with Self-Realization Fellowship. The energy level around the Village was deeply challenged. When the ministers from Ananda Village would come up to serve the folks at our little meditation group in Ashland, I could tell they were dragged down, even a bit depressed. I'm so energy sensitive that I would have picked that negativity up and not done well at all. If I'd been in the middle of all that, Ananda might have lost me for good.

I was up in Ashland when Peggy Dietz, Master's now elderly chauffeur, passed from her body. Elizabeth (now Lahari Palmer, who serves at Ananda Palo Alto) was up there helping with long-term care for Peggy. I remember knocking at the door, coming in, watching a bunch of ministers that were there ... you know, Master was there in their midst. Not only that—*all* our Masters were there. I remember saying, "They're here!" Peggy used to talk that way, too. It was palpable. It was a wonderful feeling of walking into the presence of the Masters. I sensed this presence just briefly, because then the ministers began talking, or meditating together. That's one of the earliest moments when Biraj and I got together. Biraj and I stepped out to have our own conversation. Peggy was a breath away from death, and I knew not to interrupt it. But the Masters were all there to collect her.

The Cantwell Health Food Store where I worked in Ashland was terrific. It catered to my "yuppiness." I like fine things. It was an upscale store with carpet, and all. It supplied my silver "spoon-ness." Skip Barrett worked there, too.

But alas, the assistant manager that worked there didn't like me. They just didn't like me. I don't know why. It was karmic. I would be driving home at 11:30 p.m. in my car, and I'd be crying, "What is it I don't like? Is it Cantwell's, or is it just work?" One night, driving home, crying—I was miserable—I sobbed, "Can't I just get another job?" Because I knew this one had been divinely delivered. It seemed so perfect at the beginning. When that happens, you just can't ignore it.

Buddha amidst the ivy

My apartment in the top of the barn at Buckhorn

This sweet sarcastic voice said, "Yes, you can get another job." I responded, "Terrific!"

Then the voice said, "But it has to be just like this one." "No thanks, I'll keep this one."

I thought about all the start-up time and all that misery for another two years. There were a lot of lessons in there. Most of it was about staying even minded and putting all this yogi stuff into practice. I had to stay centered—"in my spine" as we say at Ananda—in order to function.

A woman named Martha ran a fruit stand and health food store near Phoenix, Oregon, just up the road from Ashland. She would come by while I was working every once in a while, and she'd ask me, "Want to come work for me?"

I'd tell her, "Yes ... but I can't." She told me later that she only had to walk through the front door, and she could tell whether I was on duty or not, because the energy would be different. As the night manager, I ran my crew—waifs, really. They were sort of semi-homeless people.

My personal kitchen at Buckhorn

Mr. Cantwell, the owner of the store, wasn't a nice person. Toward the end of this job—though I didn't *know* it was near the end—a new person came, and Cantwell went on a vacation for two weeks. And this new person started spreading bold, outright lies. My task was to stay completely centered. I couldn't even allow a ripple in my consciousness.

It was *that* dangerous. I stayed even-minded, though. And Cantwell came back. He talked to her. He ended up firing her. And I knew at that point that I was done, that I'd passed the test. So, I asked him, "Can you let me go so that I can collect unemployment? I need a rest." And he did.

Then I collected unemployment for a while and then went to work for Martha. A women's business—there is a difference. Fruit and health foods. These women started this very successful business—probably several million dollars a year. It was right on the main road with all that action out there. Yes, it was busy. It was hard. And when all the women working for her were coming into their periods, I too would get cramps. I was that sensitive, and intuitive. And I'd say, "Get ready, it's coming. I'm getting twinges."

2000s

KRIYA YOGA

I had been living up at my old retreat grounds at Buckhorn Springs and commuting down to Ashland for work during the days. But I had gotten pneumonia, and everybody who worked at Buckhorn was gone. And I'm lying there with a 103-degree fever. Everything just seemed ugly and nasty. A couple days before, this 2nd floor apartment above the Buckhorn barn looked gorgeous, but today it seemed the worst thing I'd ever seen.

And right then, this globe floated into my vision. It was beautiful. Amidst all this ugly nasty stuff, came this soft white moon. I remember saying with a surprised gasp, "What is *that?*" And this sweet soft voice spoke. It said, "Ananda." And I go, kind of yearningly, "Ohhhh, Ananda." I started thinking of Ananda Village. And the globe said, "No, no, no. Meditation Retreat!" And I replied, "That's even better!" But this was 1999. And I didn't follow through on it right away because you can't just drop everything. These guidances come into the *right* brain. Then we still must work it over into the left brain to manifest them.

But first I had to get rid of the pneumonia. I feel like I'm dying. So, I call my friend Marilyn to come and get me. She's in town, but she's sick, too, with shingles, and she's at a doctor's appointment right then. I muster up enough strength to drive the 15 miles into Ashland. I park in front of her house and just slump there. When she comes home from the doctor's, she takes me to the hospital. Then I stayed with her for four or five days. She's in one room, moaning, and I'm in the other room, moaning.

Even after we both healed, I still had to amass the kind of money it takes to make that kind of a move. I had commitments and responsibilities. So, I plotted it out. I was meditating about how to do this.

Then one morning, I'm sitting there meditating about coming back to the Meditation Retreat, and this high squeaky voice in my head says, "Assisi." All I said was, "What do ya mean? That's in *Europe!*" I never had *any* desire to travel to Europe. But I knew I was being told to go there first. I meditated on how long I would have to stay in Assisi before I could go to the Meditation Retreat. And I came up with, "Six months."

My first stop was at Ananda Village, where I talked to Steve (later Vasanta, now deceased) Weber. He was guiding the business side of the Village at that time. I then made an appointment with Devi. I wouldn't go to Italy at that time because it was the beginning of winter, and the retreat in Assisi closes down then. I'm no fool. So, I traveled across the United States and visited friends. I visited Jan in Boulder, Colorado, Kenny & Maris Blumstein in New York. Maris is one of my soul mates, and their son Cole affectionately calls me "my guru." I stayed about a month in each place. Then I went to Florida to stay with my brother for a couple months. If I'm going to travel, I'm not going for a day or two. Only after all this did I travel to Assisi, to spend six months there.

Tempio di Luce, the meditation temple at Ananda Assisi

When I was there, I was really looking forward to getting solidly back into morning sadhana. I had really missed living in community. The community meditations were very important to me. I wanted to get back into doing my kriyas. I even had to tromp up a long hill to get to sadhana at 6 a.m. in the morning. And that isn't my favorite time. Nevertheless, every day, rain or shine, I was there. But unfortunately, I found I couldn't do my kriyas with other Italians in the room. Their policy in Ananda Assisi was to have no noise whatsoever with your kriyas. Here in America, they let you make a little noise. And my kriyas are *not* silent. It had always been difficult for me because of the muscles I had lost due to having polio as a kid. I wasn't being particularly loud, just doing kriyas the way I had always done them before in America. But I got this little tap on my shoulder, from whoever was leading sadhana that day. So, then I got very self-conscious about them, and I couldn't do them. I was going crazy, with grief.

Because I really *did* want to do my kriyas. And the best place to do them would have been in the group meditation. I was upstairs in the big temple one morning. What happens when I try to do a quiet kriya is I start to panic. It triggers something. I start gasping like I'm drowning. I was really trying to control these, and I did a kriya breath as quietly as I could. And even though I didn't make any noise, I started to have one of those panicked breathing episodes. Like an adrenaline pump—quick, short, and then you dissipate it. Kirtani Stickney (who for decades has been the co-Spiritual Director of Ananda Assisi) was sitting up in front, and she tuned in, and saw what was happening. Being very embarrassed, I roll my eyes, and think, "Oh my God . . ."

So, I think, "What am I gonna do?" Well, there's another little temple downstairs. I go into that one, but it was being used. There is another one, a tiny private little chapel, and someone was in that one, too. I think maybe I could use the bathroom stall and do my kriyas there. But you can't have someone coming into the bathroom hearing someone's loud kriya breaths! So, I found it wasn't too bad to be outside. It was March—a little brisk. But I grabbed a blanket. And there's a little pine grove on the slope next to the Assisi temple. I went up there to see if I could find a place to sit. And I saw this little statue of Jesus. I went down to that, and there was a little seat nearby. I was just thrilled. And I sat down and started doing my kriyas.

When I next looked up, there was a bubble, like the one in the Wizard of Oz that the good witch came down to earth in. The bubble kind of floated down, just like it was depicted in the movie. I suspect that whoever wrote that story must have had a true mystical experience and then tried to describe it.

There was nobody inside this bubble. It was just a shimmering bubble of cosmic energy, and it was coming down right in front of me. But I just knew that it was Babaji. It was a complete knowing. I didn't even have to ask. I can remember thinking, "I can't do these kriyas with You here. I can hardly breath!" And I went into bliss. I would sit there for a while. Then I would get this extreme desire for coffee, which was weird since I don't even *like* coffee.

I would get up. Everybody else was still in the meditation temple. And it would take me a long time to get to the dining hall, because I was barely moving—like a snail. So, I get to the dining hall finally, and I get this coffee. I sit down over near a window and put the coffee down. I'm looking out the window, and I swear I see St. Francis walking on the far ridge across the way. I'm just sitting in total bliss. Never actually drank the coffee. Didn't need it. I just needed to have something to get me to where I would see Francis. And this whole episode, including Babaji's shimmering bubble and Francis's walking by, happened every day for five straight days.

Whenever I'd sit to meditate during the days while this was going on, I would almost immediately go into bliss. I could function, but I could only handle so much of it. It was interesting. It's going to take me a lot more research—it's all still there—why I didn't just dive into it completely? I could only take it in doses. Much like what the heroine experiences in Swami's play, *Land of Golden Sunshine*.

The next week, it was pouring rain outside. I couldn't go out. The week before at these times I would go to the meditations in the temple but leave at the half time. I would just remind myself: "You know that Master was meditating for that devotee who needed Master to do his kriyas for him. Maybe he's doing a little of that for me, too." The next day, I went, and I was having a nice meditation. And I heard, "Try a kriya." And suddenly, I could do quiet kriyas, without any panic. After all that had gone on, Babaji had made it easier for me to do kriya.

That was the boon I received from Babaji's little blessing.

Mary Mintey and I had been in Gualdo Tadino, Italy ordering a gelato. I had gotten my cone, and she was getting hers. I was looking up at the TV at this interesting movie that had the World Trade Center in it, with airplanes flying into them. I assumed it was a movie because it was in Italian. I thought, "The buildings coming down and all. That's not real!" I look around and see all the Italians were staring at us, because they knew we were Americans. That's when I finally read the subscript. I thought, "Oh my God. This *isn't* a movie!" I flew back to New York City in November 2001. The whole city was in mourning from the 9/11 terrorist attacks that had just taken place.

LANDSCAPING? NOT LIKELY

I started planning to come back to the Meditation Retreat because of that vision of a globe and the guidance in 1999 that had told me it was time to return. Officially at that time, people weren't yet allowed to live up at the Meditation Retreat—for a while we called it "the Seclusion Retreat." It was illegal. There was a lot of pressure from the surrounding property owners. They felt there were too many people living up there already.

So, when I attended the weekly Meditation Group in Ashland, and told them I was going to move back to the Ananda Meditation Retreat, they said, "You can't live up *there*." And I said, "*I* can."

I'd gotten the inner green light. I just knew. It thrilled me. And at the time, I sort of knew it was a life commitment. I tried to get out of it a couple of times over the years. But it's worked out well!

When I came back at the end of 2001, the Meditation Retreat looked about the same as it had in 1997, except that the old Common Dome (which had formerly housed the kitchen and dining room) was gone. There was a huge hole where the Common Dome had been, but otherwise there was a solid wall of manzanita everywhere. And after I was here a month or two, I was out walking in the manzanita. I might even have been a little lost because the manzanita was so thick. That happened sometimes. And I asked myself, "What am I doing here? Why did I come back here? Why did You have me come back here?!"

And this sweet little voice in my head said, "You've come to finish the landscaping".

Thick clumps of manzanita bushes covered the old Meditation Retreat

And I said, "Well *that's* not likely. We *still* have no water, and no money!" We had a lot of noes. And I complained, "I don't know what that means!"

And meditating on it, and thinking about it, I thought, "Well, we could at least clear the area and make a 'canvas' for a landscaping that might come in the future." Maybe a few bushes. It would wipe the slate clean—get rid of the manzanita so that something else could happen. "Well, part of landscaping is just cleaning it up." Sort of "neatifying" the forest area and making the natural landscaping look terrific—which I thought would be good.

So, Ruth Ormondroyd, my 72-year-old friend, went into town and bought herself a tiny little chain saw less than two feet long, and we two old geezers—I was 62 at the time—started cutting down Manzanita bushes and trimming up the oak trees.

It took us a year and a half of cutting manzanita and making burn piles almost daily. We had our meals outside because you couldn't leave the piles burning. So, I'd sit by the burn pile and Ruthie would go get my supper. Or she'd sit by the burn pile, and I'd go get her lunch. We just sat out there on upturned buckets and conducted "fire ceremonies". We had a couple of workdays when folks from Ananda Village came up and cleared real big thickets with us. And in about a year and a half it was cleared. I thought it looked nice. Actually, it looked terrific. It was finally "landscaped!"

Four workmates in 2002

BABAJI APPEARS

Throughout 2002 and much of 2003, Ruth and I had been half of the crew that was running the Meditation Retreat. There were only four: Narada Agee (who was a fine electrician, now deceased), Sahaja Simms (who in 2022 became the newest manager up at the Meditation Retreat) and the two of us. Haridas and Roma had been our bosses before that but had been re-assigned. We were managed by Steve (later Vasanta) Weber at the time, but his office over at Ananda Village was too far away from the Meditation Retreat to have much day-to-day influence.

Soon Ram Smith (now serving at Ananda Village) and Dhyana were made Spiritual Directors up at the Retreat. They would come up frequently but weren't here all the time. The Retreat had lost the Living Discipleship program for some time before that, but Ram and Dhyana brought it back. That program was a great way to serve, and helped to boost the energy up here, as well as being a money-maker for us. We had a wonderful year and a half with Ram and Dhyana as our guides. They were very special. Ram started talking about, "We need some ponds and plants up here."

I said, "No way, Ram. This is not SRF's Lake Shrine. None of that can work up here. We have no water." It was just a hot, dry mountaintop. Our well was doing a mere seven or eight gallons a minute, but that had to supply the whole Retreat—all the guests, the shower houses, and the group kitchen—with water.

He kept persisting, and he came out of the temple one day, and said, "I saw Babaji sitting on top of our old root cellar."

We responded incredulously, "*Sure* you did!"

But Dhyana said, "No, it's *true!*"

Ram said, "Babaji wants us to turn the root cellar into a meditation cave."

We said, "Ram, that's just not likely". We were storing our garbage in there at the time to keep it away from the bears. Garbage would just not be an appropriate environment for Babaji. We complained, "Where would we keep the garbage?" It took us about half an hour to realize that what we were hearing from Ram *was* true guidance. Finally, we dropped everything and found a little shed to stick the garbage in and cleaned out the underground concrete storage room that was to become Babaji's Cave. There was a group of Living Discipleship students up here at the time, so all of us scrubbed and cleaned and painted, and got it all done. And it looked quite nice—on the inside.

Babaji's Cave Meditation Space

But outside, the old root cellar still looked like a bomb shelter, or an ammunition dump—like you'd see out in the Nevada desert—with its straight wooden sides and little wisps of grass on top. It didn't help that a big tractor had recently knocked down the old Common Dome that had been just alongside of the root cellar. That had left a big gaping hole in the ground. Nischala Cryer pointed out to us that the Vedic scriptures say that wherever there's been a holy temple, or holy area, if you fill it with water, water is said to retain those vibrations that all those years the former building had given to the area.

And so I called Prakash Van Cleave, our tractor guy, and said, "Could you come and push up a little dirt? We'll make a little fishpond." I figured it wouldn't need much dirt to do that. So, I set him loose, while I drove on a town trip for supplies. Since we work on guidance up here, and Prakash is a deep devotee, I trusted that he, too, would get guidance. I just left him alone to decide how best to disguise the bomb shelter. When I came back a couple hours later, I discovered that Prakash had dug this *huge* hole, with all these mounds of dirt all over the place. And I thought, "Oh, wow, I was thinkin' of a little pond, no more than 12 feet across. What're we gonna do with *this?*" We decided we would just fill the hole very slowly with water and do a simple landscaping around it. That was the beginning of Babaji's pond.

We spent only $200 to renovate Babaji's Cave. But we spent it before we ever asked permission from our bosses. When the project had already been completed, Steve Weber announced he was coming over from the Management Office. Ram fretted that Steve was coming to find out where his $200 went. But I told Ram, "Don't worry. Swami says intuition is stronger than institution!"

Babaji's Pond when it was brand new, 2004

Mantradevi LoCicero's painting of Babaji's Pond

Babaji close-up

Babaji's Pond now, with its lively school of goldfish

New Annapurna dining hall that Haridas Blake and Nakula Cryer put up

The frogs just showed up

Nischala Cryer, garden visionary

NISCHALA AND NAKULA

So, one of the first "landscaping" we did was to fill Babaji's pool and add plants to the mounds of dirt that had been pushed up all around the new hole. This was early in 2004. Someone came along and gave us a liner that would fit in that space, and so we got the pond in place. Nakula and Nischala Cryer gave us a bunch of seed money to start. They gave us $7,000, which at the time was an astronomical amount. So, we could put in a little garden around that pond, and a tiny bit more over by the new Annapurna dining hall. At the time, we thought that was all there would be. This was the very beginning of the Meditation Retreat Garden. The whole thing sure has grown over the years, but slowly. Every fall now, years after Babaji's pond was first started, I must take out at least half of the surrounding plants because it grows so lush there.

I might mention that when this pond started, we put the *fish* in, but we didn't put the frogs in. The frogs just showed up. I mean, the first day we filled that pond with water, four or five dragonflies showed up – the most beautiful dragonflies. There was a russet colored one, and there was a green one, and a blue one, just out of nowhere. The frogs hopped in from somewhere. But this mountaintop is surrounded by miles of near desert. So where could the frogs have come from?

They bring an awful lot of delight to people. I see more people tracking down these frogs than are even looking at the flowers. Especially the young people—the little boys and little girls—love to check out these frogs. But almost everybody who goes over there, walks around that pond, and the frogs jump in or sit and look at them. People are always over there enjoying those frogs.

Babaji's Pond is also the spot where Mantradevi painted that wonderful painting of hers.

Nakula, being a building contractor, had just completed the construction of the new dining room which Haridas had begun as a replacement for the rickety old Common Dome. That dining room took five years of Nakula's weekends, sometimes one piece of plywood at a time (which had been all the funds that could be raised that week) and using all-volunteer labor.

Around this time, Nischala and Nakula had the expansive idea to start up a brand-new institute of higher education over in Sonoma County. But very soon, Swami, Jyotish and Devi all pleaded with them, "Why don't you do whatever you want, but do it here at the Meditation Retreat, instead." So, the first academic programs started here late in 2003, until gradually a full-fledged undergraduate four-year college—The Ananda College—sprang up at the Meditation Retreat, grown by Nischala and Nakula's patient and persistent efforts. The college was housed at the Meditation Retreat for eight years.

But I let Nischala and Nakula know right away that I didn't give two hoots about the college. "My loyalty is to the *Retreat*," I told them. I meant that I supported the college, but my main focus would always be the Retreat. And they were fine with that.

I think Jyotish and Devi realized that the Retreat staff wasn't yet convinced that having the college move into the Meditation Retreat was such a great idea, so they invited the four of us to come meditate with them in Swami's original dome. At the end of the meditation together, I whispered to Devi, "Now I feel it's OK for the college to come. I got in meditation that they were coming to fix the infrastructure up here."

Devi whispered back, "I got the same thing!"

There were a lot of beginnings to this garden. Nischala and Nakula envisioned a *big* garden. But it wasn't until they supplied that original infusion of money that it really took off. It was a desire of theirs that if they were going to put the Ananda College campus up here, then it ought to look a little better. The land there was almost chokingly stark. Once we had taken down all the underbrush, it looked a little severe, flat, and boring. Nischala appreciated what we were doing. Before that, all of us had been thinking small. Obviously Divine Mother *wasn't* thinking small. Anyway, now we began in an even bigger way.

Nischala described it later on in this way: "There were some things that I heard Swami say. 'The west needs to have more of Divine Mother's energy.' He said, 'The way that women can do that is to do gardening. Gardens bring in the feminine energy.' I was really hearing that. And all four of us talked. Nakula and I took Charles and Ruth over to Mendocino to see the Mendocino Botanical Gardens. They're beautiful. And that was our inspiration at first."

She went on, "Charles and I worked really well together. When Charles and I get together, the ideas grow. He was a natural ally. It was like two fellow artists—I'm an artist, and he's a *plant* artist. Both Charles and I always work from intuition, so we were in tune with each other. I would come up to him and say, 'Charles, what do you think about blah blah blah.' And he would go away, then three or four days later he would come back and say, 'I thought about it, and . . .' That's how Charles and I worked."

As I (Charles) mentioned earlier, landscaping, gardening and plants runs in my blood. I come from a line of gardeners and farmers. My mother was Italian, my grandmother ran an orchard, and I ended up going to the University of Florida taking ornamental horticulture and landscape design. So, I actually do have credentials for doing this, although by the time I started this project, those credentials had long since been put away. I never in a million years would have taken on this project. It wasn't beyond my abilities, but it was beyond what I would have chosen to do. Yet the guidance was so strong. You can't turn up your nose at that.

I knew all the techniques. I knew how deep to dig the holes, and how to plant the plants and all of that. But I let "Mother"—the Divine one—guide all the rest. The "I" part of me tried to stay as little involved as possible, as if "I" was becoming "we." I kept focused on just enjoying the labor.

People often ask me how I decide where to put all these paths at the Retreat? Well, sometimes I watch where people are going. Sometimes I'll walk it myself. I'm standing here and I want to get over to there. How am I going to get there? Then I sort of know where people are going to go. I don't like straight paths. Straight lines don't occur much in nature. The left-brain tends to get excited by them, but I think it's really the right-brain that knows how to get off this planet. It's the right-brain that knows all *else* is a delusion. So, it's the most fun when I merely intuit what goes where.

Most of what's happening up here in the Retreat Garden is through guidance. You can identify true guidance when there is a sweetness to it; it flows, and it tends to work. If it's taking a lot of work to get it going, stop and ask for guidance.

The way I had been doing this garden is mostly by listening. Though sometimes I see lines on the ground. I know I'm usually the only one that can see them, but all of a sudden there'd be lines, and I would look and usually say, "Uh-oh", because I knew there must be something else getting ready to happen here. So, it kept expanding, and I kept thinking, "This is getting awfully *big!*"

We had no idea exactly where this was going, except the hint from that booming voice back in 1993 that shouted in my head, "I said *six* feet! This is going to be a place of pilgrimage!" So, it is going to be a special place to come. *Pilgrimage* means that you come, and you are uplifted.

You've probably heard of Medjugorje, the place in the former Yugoslavia where Mother Mary has been appearing for over thirty years on a regular basis, giving messages. It's very much like Fatima or Lourdes. Mother Mary was appearing to six children. And the children asked her early on, "Why did you pick us?"

And she answered, "I don't always pick my best."

And I thought, "That explains a lot." That's how I feel about why I got chosen to do this garden. Though, I do know I have a particular talent. Some people can sing. Partly, I got to do this because I could ... *hear*. And, I was *willing* to follow through on what I heard.

St. Francis statue that Clara Evans installed, 1992

The Twelve Apostles

Cross on the Jesus Tree

SAINT FRANCIS CIRCLE AND THE JESUS TREE

The Saint Francis area had been created honoring two things. Saint Francis, of course, but also honoring Clara Evans. She had built that original little Saint Francis Shrine. She actually had a little garden up here when I came in 1993. She was the first one who started cutting back the manzanita, even before Ruth and I did. And when I got here, it had been mandated that she had to take her garden out, because it was going to use water that they didn't have. She was perhaps already in the process of moving away. When they started to dismantle that area, I said, "Would you just leave that. This woman has worked so hard." So, we kept it from being destroyed. But that little shrine just sat there practically all by itself from 1993 until 2004.

That little circle of evergreens straight across the path from Saint Francis was done in the second wave of landscaping, in 2004. I was digging out over around the Babaji Pond and found that big rock. And I looked at it and said to myself, "That's a nice rock. That's a seat. Where am I going to put this rock?"

And that big tree across the path from the Francis statue is where I took it. Not because the tree itself had any significance. I just thought it would be a good place to meditate. Not overly excited about it because it was right on the main path. I just thought I wanted to mirror that image across the path, so that you'd sit there, and look right at St. Francis. Before all the other bushes grew up, you looked past St. Francis and looked all the way to Babaji.

So, we ended up mirroring Clara's work that she had done previously on the St. Francis shrine.

That's when I put those little evergreen trees in. I wasn't paying any attention that I had put twelve of them in. Only recently did I get reports about unusual things starting to happen there. I hadn't promoted that spot. I'd put them in and forgot about them. When I ordered those trees, I wanted them to be fairly high, but when they arrived, they were little, short things. I was very disappointed. It's taken 20 years for them to grow up to the height they are now, where they are becoming something special.

In 2018, a woman says she was sitting there, and Jesus came to her. And she says, "Those trees standing around became the twelve apostles." Thereafter, she called it the Jesus Tree, which I think is very appropriate since it's right across from St. Francis.

I can tell when something's true, by the feeling that comes when I think about it. Otherwise, I would normally say something like, "That's nice." But something happened there. I never knew what was happening. It had been like a puzzle. I had put those in but had to experience later why I had done that. For a long time in the garden tours I give, I never talked about that spot except maybe to point to it briefly. There is so much to talk about, I just never included this one, until recently.

GRANDFATHER TREE

When we first put in a little bit of the garden in 2004, I would plant some plants, but I would have to water it two or three times a day. We could water, and 15-20 minutes later, it would be sucked bone dry. The oak tree roots would invade and instantly suck it dry. It was like there was a battle going on. By this time, our garden surrounded Babaji pond, and a little bit in front of the dining room. This battle went on for two years. I was cutting oak roots, trying to protect the new plantings. I was Findhorn-trained, so I should have known better. I was being stubborn and very dense. I didn't even hear them—instead I was in battle with them! Then this psychic came in, and told me, "Your garden is very lovely, but the oak trees are quite upset."

As soon as he said that, instantly I knew. It just came to me, clearly, as if I were watching a movie. Boom! I knew! We had talked to everything else we had been dealing with, but we hadn't talk to these oak trees. Celia was here—she's called Jayashree now. She was an administrator at the Ananda College. I noticed that butterflies would come and land on Jayashree's hand. I figure if the *butterflies* trust her, so should *we*. She really wanted to help. So, we started talking to these oak trees, apologizing, bowing, kowtowing, anything we could think of. It was two long years of this. Don't tell me nature is not vindictive!

Grandfather Tree

By this time, the whole top of our hill was cleared of manzanita. I walked home the same way every day, past what's now Mother's Pond, and cut across to my former residence in Renunciation Cabin from there. One day in Spring 2005 while I was walking home, for some reason I abruptly stopped, turned, and looked to my right. And there was the biggest oak tree that I had ever seen. And I said, "Where did *that* come from?" I 'd never seen that tree before. Even today, if I don't point it out, hardly anybody notices it. There's a path less than five feet from this tree, yet none of the monks or others who lived down below the hill from it seemed to have had any idea that it was there. It's like in that book, *Mists of Avalon*, where there was a sacred area that remained shrouded. This giant tree was obscured by sheer energy. It just didn't want to be seen. Not until we were ready, and perhaps, not until we had apologized enough. I was startled to see that tree. It would be as if I turned in the middle of a workday, and someone who lived in the San Francisco Bay Area was suddenly standing here beside me. And what came out of my mouth, was "Grandfather!" No thought—that's just what popped out. And I said, "Well, *that's* a good name for that tree."

So Jayashree and I sat for some time with Grandfather, and all the invasions stopped. After two years of hugging and bowing, sitting with Grandfather was the only thing that changed things. It changed very quickly. The invasions had all been punishment for not realizing the correct order of things. This is not only an oak forest, but a *sacred* oak forest. Oak groves were sacred to Native Americans. And we hadn't asked permission. We just barged in and did it. We hadn't talked to the main oak tree when we were causing all that disruption. Yes, we had been talking to the manzanita bushes that we had been cutting down. But it would be the same as if we came to your house while you were away, and rearranged everything and changed the colors, and didn't ever ask permission from you, the owner. I wouldn't think you would be very pleased when you got home, especially if I had picked day-glow for the walls. This was a good example of the need for cooperation with nature. After we started talking to Grandfather, everything calmed down. Oak roots don't invade our garden anymore.

These trees are as big as any that exist around here. There are a lot of old oaks out and about that are all falling down. Many are at the end of their cycles, broken and dying. But Grandfather (and "Grandmother" on the other side of our garden) are as old as anything up here—they could be 400 years old. They're a bit craggy, but still healthy. I think it's because they're on power spots.

We put a big rock at the base of Grandfather that you can sit on. It's got a little concave shape—I call it a soft rock—so you can comfortably get your back up against the tree. Trees—big trees especially—have electromagnetic energy, and it's oriented up and down. And if you sit with them, and you put your back against them, it lines up your electromagnetic energy, in much the same way that some of our breathing exercises and Kriya do. These big trees line your energy up. This is why people oftentimes sit with their backs to trees. You feel it—wise, loving. It can put thoughts in your head. The whole garden is bracketed by these two strong tree energies, Grandfather and Grandmother.

Did I ever sense any words from Grandfather? Some of the time you get guidance—just enough to get started. I'm not overly curious. That quality used to drive my mother crazy. My old pal Ruthie was the curious one up here at the Retreat. If I wanted to know anything like that, I would ask Ruth. No, when I sat with Grandfather early on, it was like being in the old book section of the library. I'd get that musty smell, and cobwebby, craggy feel. He doesn't talk much. But you can have satsang with him. You can pick up his energy. I would get information. Like he would put a book in your hand but wasn't going to explain it. I never remember getting any thoughts in my head from him, but remember ... I'd been busy. There's hardly ever time to sit and dwell on anything but the general feeling. I experience this garden as a whole, all mixing together.

But if you are set on conversing, try talking to the younger oaks. They're a little more vocal.

So, Ruth and I were here for 2004. It was about the end of '04 that I got guidance about needing to go to Assisi, and to take Ruthie. So, we were going to go in '05. We started planning that. But as it was getting closer, Jyotish and Devi called Ruth and me to a meeting and asked if we wouldn't stay to support Nischala and Nakula in their new project. It was quite a shock. We had been chomping to get out of here. I just prayed, "I need to learn to do what Ananda needs. We are living at Ananda. Is this OK if we don't go to Italy now?" I knew there were lessons for both of us in going. The reply came, "Yes, it's OK. The lessons will just be a little more difficult." Meaning, if we had gone to Italy then, the lessons would have been easier.

I ended up having to spend a year in the Meditation Retreat kitchen. I had to totally let go of the garden, because there was nobody to do the kitchen. Nischala *did* want the garden to happen, but it made no difference. We had no one in the kitchen. I had to turn my back on the garden. But first I asked inwardly if it was OK for me to leave the garden to handle the kitchen. The answer I got back was, "It's OK."

I was the only one around who understood kitchens—the ordering and the buying and all of that—from my time in the U.N. Plaza restaurant. At that time, the garden only consisted of Babaji's pond and right in front of the dining building. We were only about a year and a half into the project. I didn't worry about the garden at all, other than an occasional question, or watching over the watering system, but minimal. So, I ran the Retreat kitchen for a year.

Running the Meditation Retreat kitchen, 2005

THE DEER AND THE TURKEYS

When we put in the original garden, the one with Babaji's Pond and the little garden around it, the deer had really stayed away. I had been involved earlier with that Findhorn community in Massachusetts. *They* had a garden, and the deer didn't eat *it*, so I figured if the deer are not going to eat their garden, they're not going to eat *ours*. And they didn't—for the *first* year.

Then something happened. 2005 was the height of one of California's recurring droughts. There was no food out there for them that summer, so they started eating everything. They even ate stuff that they really didn't like. They were devouring this garden. And it doesn't take much devouring by deer before plants don't revive. They don't grow back. I ought to have been able to commune with these things. I should have been able to keep the deer out that way. Instead, I felt so badly for them. They really were getting awfully hungry during that long drought. I was using deer spray. It's awfully smelly stuff, and it tastes awful, too. But it seemed like salad dressing to them. They were coming right behind me, munching. "Oh, geez," I say to myself.

Then, when we three were brainstorming, Nakula said, "What if we create a three-acre space around the temple and the dining room, and fence it all in?" It was Nakula, himself, who drew up designs for the gates and the little arboretum that you pass through. Just then Ruthie came forward and gave us the money that we needed to put up the deer fencing. And it wasn't a small donation—$14,000—because we didn't want the fence in so close where it would intrude on the feeling of the garden. The fence had to go way out, so that you're not aware that you are fenced in. It was going to take quite a bit of money. It worked. There are no more deer munching on our garden.

At the same time, we talked to the deer. We told them what we were going to do. I had talked to them before. The *deer* were pretty good. They really had tried. Except when they got so hungry.

The hungry Ananda deer

However, occasionally the *turkeys* would fly over the new fence, and they chomped on things, too. And I would talk to these turkeys, and talk again to these turkeys, and then I'd be in meditation in the morning, and I'd talk even *there* to these turkeys. They *halfway* listened, but they were obstinate. I had a little fig tree. It had six figs on it. One day I came out of the dining hall, and I thought, "I've been nurturing these figs, watching them grow and plump out, and turn a nice color. I wonder if those turkeys ate those figs?" And I went over there – no figs!

Now previously when we would chase these turkeys – they'd only run twenty feet, then they'd stop and look back at you. They knew we weren't going to hurt them. This day, I go over there, and there's no figs, and I shouted, "Where did my figs go?" And I look up, and further than a football field—you know, 100 yards—they were way over by Happiness Lodge (formerly Kali Lodge.) These three turkeys were going flat out! They looked like Road Runner, with their necks straight out in front, and their feet just churning, going flat out! And I had to laugh out loud, because those turkeys *knew* they'd eaten my figs, and they knew they were in *big* trouble.

Now, the next morning, in meditation, I said to myself, "That's it, turkeys!" I said, "We have a good friend over in North San Juan. One-armed John." And I said, "He *loves* to eat turkey. And he has a *big* gun!" I said, "The next intrusion into this garden, I'm calling *John*." You know, those turkeys stopped. From then on, they would go around. You *can* communicate with nature.

We had a fire not long ago that was swooping up the hill toward the Expanding Light retreat. In response, disciples were sitting on the lawn, chanting, and meditating. And a fireman came and said to them, "I don't know what you all are doing, but please keep it up! I've never seen a fire act like this. It gets to where it's ready to swoop into a group of buildings, and then abruptly changes its course." So, our focused thoughts can affect what happens in the future.

In my garden tours now, I include a section about consciousness, that everything around us, even the gravel we're standing on, has consciousness. And consequently, you could communicate even with that. My guru Yogananda said that the easiest place to find God is in nature. I think I've come to understand why. I believe it's because God uses the same frequency that Nature does. Remember the old radios that had dials you'd use to tune them in? Well, the frequency that we communicate on with Nature is the same frequency that the Divine uses. So, once you can communicate with Nature, it's a very small step to include the Divine.

Ruth Ormondroyd with her daughter & Charles

BACK TO INDIA, AND ASSISI

By the end of October 2005, it really *was* time to take a break. Ruthie and I finally took our long-postponed trip to Italy. But when we got there, turned out "there was no room at the inn." It would have been fine if we had been able to afford $70 a night at their retreat, but we couldn't. So, we took an apartment with a close friend three miles away. But then we had no way of getting back and forth from that apartment to the center at Il Refugio. It was very isolating. And then it got cold, and we only had a wood burning cooking stove for heat.

So, at the end of 2005, we went into town and booked tickets to India. We started at Varkala Beach, and Amma's ashram, and the Periyar Wildlife Sanctuary—all in Kerala, southern India. On the way out of the Wildlife Sanctuary, we were lamenting that we hadn't seen any wild elephants, when just then, right by the road was a small family group. One bull who started to charge us with his ears flapping and his trunk making threatening gestures. We were only 50 feet away and ready to jump back in the jeep and get out of there. But luckily, he stopped short. There was a baby in the group—the cutest little thing—along with a teenager and four mamas. These paid no attention to us, eating their way placidly through the forest and along the creek. I guess they knew papa would take care of them. We trailed this herd for about 45 minutes—one of the highlights of the whole India trip.

We had a real adventure when we took the "Chicken Bus" through Tamil Nadu on the way to Madurai. This trip took place at night on a two-way road no wider than the bus itself. The road, when there was a road, was all twisty with a cliff on one side, a mountain on the other and no shoulders. Big buses and trucks loaded to the gills—as were we—kept coming at us out of the night. We seemed to get passed them with only centimeters to spare. Sometimes we met them head-on, going top speed, then stopped four inches from each other before deciding who was going to back up. Four hours came and went, and we were not even halfway through this trip from hell. We finally reached the flatlands and stopped briefly in a busy city.

The driver said we had ten minutes, so Ruth and I headed off to pee. When we got back, no bus! It had left with all of our luggage, but without us. What to do? Then a man grabbed us, yelling in a language we didn't understand, frantically pointing down the road to a departing bus. We immediately chase this bus, weaving through traffic, cars, auto rickshaws, and cows, trying to catch this bus which by now was picking up speed. Ruth fell behind, but I sprinted ahead and grabbed at the door of the bus and swung myself inside, screaming, "Stop the bus! Wait for Madam!" (That's what they call Ruth in India.) They all looked at me like I was crazy, until I noticed it was not our bus. At this point, the bus was traveling about 20 miles an hour, but I jumped off anyway. I was running down the middle of the road, weaving through traffic searching for Ruth, when half-way back to the station our *real* bus passed me and there was no sign of Ruth anywhere. When I finally got back to the bus stand, I was thinking where to find Ruth, when a bus pulled out going to Madurai. I jumped on thinking that one of us needed to get there and protect our luggage—that was our lifeline. I figured that Ruth would get to Madurai somehow. I hoped and prayed that she had gotten on the right bus, and that it would be delayed and that the bus that I was on would arrive early.

As it turned out, Ruth was on the right bus, because as she ran by the correct bus chasing the wrong bus, people started to yell and point at the right bus. She ran through all the traffic and was pulled on the right bus just in the nick of time, wondering where *I* was going on *my* bus.

This trip, that was supposed to take four and one-half hours, actually took eight hours.

But the power of prayer can be astounding. Ruth's bus arrived 20 minutes late, with my bus arriving 20 minutes early. So, after being on different buses for hours, the two of us arrived at our destination at precisely the same time!

There was a cute detail here. When my bus pulled in, Ruthie was sitting atop our luggage, fending off the rickshaw drivers who were trying to be a little too helpful, as Indian drivers are wanting to be. She looked up, saw me, and I've never in my whole life seen a person happier to see me!

Soon afterwards we spent a week at the foot of Mt. Arunachala and Ramana Maharshi's ashram. One of the best meditations I ever had was in Ramana Maharshi's second cave atop Mt. Arunachala. I could have stayed there forever. There was a spring right next to it, just pouring down water. It had a hut built up against a hollow part in the cave, and somehow all the workmanship was done to perfection. Everything about it was so relatable. I was just in bliss.

Next, we spent another week in Sai Baba's ashram in Puttaparthy. Later we went north to the beach in Goa, then ten days at the Ananda Ashram in Gurgaon. Then we visited Pushkar in Rajasthan, visited all the shrines associated with Yogananda and Ramakrishna around Calcutta and Serampore, and stayed two weeks in Rishikesh's Lakshman Jula, plus I took a side trip up to visit the Dalai Lama in Dharamshala.

One of the highlights for me was getting to visit Sri Yukteswar's ashram in Serampore. We met up with the students from Ananda College, who were on pilgrimage there at the same time. The man conducting our tour said, "You want to meditate in his bedroom?" Ya, of course! So, we went upstairs to get to the bedroom. I have been enamored with Sri Yukteswar's balcony ever since I was in what we had called Monastic Training. I had even wanted to build a replica of it myself. So, while I was walking across it on the way to the bedroom, I'm going, "Wow, *this* is it!" The rest of the group went on into the bedroom, but I just stopped, put my hands on the railing, took a breath, and looked down into what remained of the old courtyard. And I said to myself, "Oh, I know this energy. It's extremely familiar. Oh, my goodness, it's the same thing I feel when I'm in the places where St. Francis prayed at Assisi!" This was the same balcony we read about in the *Autobiography of a Yogi,* and see visually in the *Awake* movie, when Yukteswar calls out, "Mukunda, I *know* how you are meditating. Come here." And he puts young Yogananda into samadhi. It's *that* balcony.

Oh, one side benefit of traveling in India: Ever since my stay there, I don't seem to mind messes nearly so much.

Our trip through India took four months of 2006. On our return from India, we stopped off in Italy, where our buddy Mary Mintey put us up. Same thing happened in Italy this time that had happened to me when I returned to Ananda Village in 2001. Back then, all the people that I had known from before had left, and the minister in charge of membership didn't know me from Adam. She treated me as if I were a raw recruit, and I had to jump through all the hoops once again. The same thing happened in Italy in 2006. This time it was Arjuna and Shivani Lucki who didn't know me from Adam. They were going to put us into a tent. Mary laid down the law to them. She told them, "Charles and Ruthie are going to stay in *my* house." Ruth in the main bedroom, me in the spare bedroom, and Mary on the couch. It lasted that way for only a couple of weeks because Ruthie got so sick that right away, she had to return home to America.

I did get to do a lot of gardening there for the rest of 2006, which is probably why I was inwardly told to go over to Italy in the first place. They had lost their gardener—Reena, a fiery gal. If I had gotten there earlier, I probably could have prevented a lot of what was happening from happening. They had a young English guy in his late 20's named Matthew that didn't know a lot about gardening, and he was tearing her garden out and putting what he thought should be there—little formal Englishy stuff. One time Reena grabbed a butcher knife in the kitchen and was heading into the dining room toward this guy, when the staff tackled her. He'd been messing with her garden, and what he was doing really *wasn't* appropriate.

This guy, Matthew, didn't much care for me since he thought of me as usurping his bailiwick. But I had the natural authority of having more experience. Suddenly, I was given this huge budget, because Swami was coming for some kind of big event. The young guy couldn't figure out how I got all these thousands of Euros approved. We were buying plants and getting things all over the place. Ananda had just bought the property next door. The side of the path that went to the temple had been the edge of our property before. The professor who had owned that property wouldn't let us put so much as a rock on his property. But now we had bought it. What the young guy was doing was ripping out Reena's big forsythia hedge to make more room. But you shouldn't just rip out what someone else has done. What *did* make sense was to move the hedge back three feet and break it up by interspersing it with some lilacs. So, we started doing that. Soon, Matthew and I were discussing some point in the dining hall and Reena comes in, and instantly Matthew turned completely white with fear. Belligerently Reena challenges, "Who is *doing* that?"

And matter-of-factly I say, "That was me."

And she says meekly, "Oh, OK."

That didn't improve my relationship with Matthew. At one point, he says to me, "Well I don't like that plant."

I said, "It doesn't make any difference what you like and what you don't like. It's about what *works!*" I think he learned a lot that year.

WHISPERS FROM YUKTESWAR

We had always heard that the Meditation Retreat was on American Indian sacred ground. But we never knew why. While putting the garden in, I think I discovered why. There are little palpable energy spots here and there all over the top of this mountain, like at Sedona. You can feel them. If it had been water, each spring would have had a slightly different taste. Each spring of energy has a slightly different feel to it. We've tried to match up statues with the energy that is theirs. Mother's Pond—because the energy there is unconditionally loving—that's where you go to get a hug. But a no-nonsense spot, that's where we put in Sri Yukteswar. Grandfather's spot is wise and impersonally loving. Every place that you see statues and benches are places that have been identified as having energy. The Babaji Pond is a place you can get your batteries charged.

For instance, there is a sweet spot right in front of the big statue of Mother Mary. John Grieves (a disciple from South Africa) and I were putting that path in, it was probably 9 pm at night. We had been working for 14 hours straight, even eating while we were working, because I was directing a rented Bobcat tractor that had to be taken back the next morning. We stopped for a minute and got off the tractor. And I told him, "John, step back a little bit." He moved back.

He said, "What just happened?"

"Now step forward." What a difference! It was like having delicious honey poured all over you. You just felt this wave of joy. And that one's not even marked! It's in front of, and a little to the left of, the statue. There's another sweet spot in the fruit orchard that's not yet marked. It actually drains away anxiety. You might ask whether I ever go over to those spots and feel them sometimes? No, I've been busy. Mother doesn't give me that kind of time very often.

Just sit in these spots. The trick is to sit in these spots and see what you feel. Not what you think, but what you feel. When you die, the thinking brain dies, all the equations, and the facts. What remains with you is your consciousness. What you have learned in your heart, you take *that* with you. Due to past lives, it's so hard to know what you're actually dealing with. Have you ever run into someone who you just instantly liked, or disliked? Most likely, that's coming from past lives.

It's relentless here. Divine Mother is always asking stuff of us. This Retreat heals—not the physical—but the psychological, emotional, and spiritual. It does it by poking at you. It finds where you've got a button—those issues that are burning a hole in your soul. Like a hot rock, you have to get rid of it. All you have to do is let it go. You don't have to understand it. You don't need to know what it's all about. But first you must let it go. *After* letting it go, only then can you analyze it. *That's* the kind of energy that is up here.

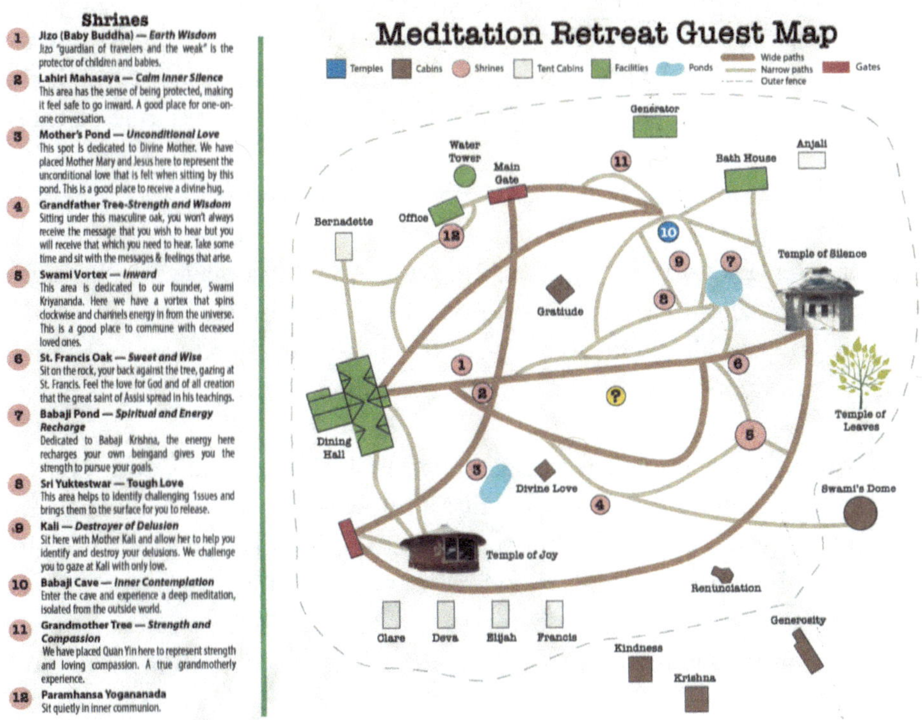

Early on, there were these two patches of the garden, the one by the temple, the other all the way over by the dining hall. The oak roots had stopped attacking. We had gotten the trees limbed up nicely, but otherwise the middle area between the two major gardens had nothing but leaves scattered all over the ground. I'm thinking, "There needs to be a little bit of green—a bit of transition—to connect between the temple and the dining room gardens." Whenever I would pass between the old office dome and the shower houses, I would hear a whisper, that would say simply, "Special, special". I knew there was something going on there, but I was busy. I figured that there was probably a shrine trying to happen there. Besides, it didn't tell me what to put in. And I thought, "Well, it will eventually, and *then* I'll know what to do."

That's normally how I locate the shrines because you can't decide intellectually, "I'm going to put a shrine here." There has to be the right energy there for a shrine. It isn't by chance that Swami chose to put the old common dome and the temple on these Retreat grounds. The energy flowing up under that spot is so strong that it flows back down the hill right into Swami's Dome. When Dhyana was staying there, she had to keep the back door closed so she wouldn't get so wired. Later, we put a wooden fence across that area to help divert some of the energy toward other parts of the mountain. So, we try to locate the shrine areas where there's one of those springs.

One day walking by the "special, special" area, I sort of saw a little water feature in the middle, and I thought, "Well, *that* would be nice." A couple months later, I was in the feed store in town, and I saw a cattle trough, made of nice material, a nice shape, good depth—otherwise raccoons would be able to clean out all the mosquito fish. It was perfect. I had some donation money with me. "How much?" I asked the salesclerk.

"$95."

I started to reach into my pocket. Then I said, "No, there's some plants I need to buy." Then I'm thinking, "I don't know if maybe I'm making all this stuff up." There is such a thin line between true guidance and egoic thought. "Maybe I'm conjuring all this. Maybe it's my ego making it up, and it's not from guidance at all. So, I'm not going to do it. If this is supposed to happen, someone has to put a $100 bill in the palm of my hand!" No one ever does that, right?

Four days later, Satya (the ship's sailor who was the first man back in the late 1960's to live over the winter at the Meditation Retreat) said, "Hold out your hand." And he put a $100 bill in the palm of my hand, and added, "This is for the garden".

And I think, "Uh-oh, now I have to dig that hole!"

Everything here has been by donation. The Retreat has never had a regular budget for this stuff. It's all just through the goodness of people's hearts. I've sometimes used my Social Security retirement check to buy a few extra plants that I wanted for the garden, but that never would've been enough. Otherwise, it's all from other people's donations.

However, I didn't get back to the feed store in town for weeks. I was busy! When I finally got back to the store, those troughs were all gone. A new style was there, and *that* style wouldn't have worked. I asked, "What happened to the other troughs you had for sale?

The salesperson answered, "Some man came in this morning and bought them all."

And I think, "Oh, I should have come in right away. When you get guidance, you need to act." I was beating myself up. As I was leaving the store, suddenly I had an insatiable desire to find out what was behind this large piece of cardboard leaning up against a distant building. It felt a lot like when Yogananda was looking for those stained-glass windows for Hollywood Church. So, I peeked behind the cardboard, and there was the exact trough I needed. I went back into the salesperson, and said, "There is still one there."

He said, "No there's not."

I said, "Come."

When he saw it, he said, "OK, I'll give you that one for half price." So, I brought it home, and I set it down haphazardly. There was nothing but leaves all around. I hadn't yet had time to select just the right spot for the water feature. I was busy.

You can't feel the energy of these places until you sit down and get quiet. You can walk past a hundred times and perceive nothing. It's not until you are quiet and receptive that you pick it up. So, I had the trough setting nearby, waiting for when I had time to site it properly.

We had a man, Jagrav Quinn (he now runs Radio Ananda) who was working up at the Retreat with us. He had been very serviceful.[8] He was always doing extra things, raking, and picking up sticks. This was going to be the last day he was to work with us, and I was in the middle of doing the town run for groceries. And I thought, "Rats, I could have had him dig that hole!" You know, I don't like to dig these big holes. It wouldn't have worked to call him to try to tell him where to dig the hole. The trough wasn't sitting in the right place, and these things are very specific.

So, when I got home, Jagrav comes up to me and kind of shyly says, "I don't know if I did right, but I had a very strong desire to dig that hole."

I hadn't really talked to him about it except to say "Someday . . ." I said to myself, "Charles, smile. Look happy. He did a great service. He dug the hole, even though you *know* it's in the wrong spot!" We walked over to the site, and it was *perfect!* Everything about it was perfect.

And that's how the shrine to Sri Yukteswar came about. It has the no-nonsense, direct, tell-it-like-it-is energy. This is where you sit if you want *that* kind of breakthrough. You know, Sri Yukteswar does not suffer fools lightly. He gives you an indication of what you need to do and expects you're going to do it.

Yukteswar Shrine

It's like if you've got a jar of pond water, the top will be clear, but the bottom will have a layer of silt. It's those particles of silt that are the issues that we carry from life to life to life. And they just sit there, until the jar is disturbed. An event can disturb it, person can disturb it, your mother can disturb it. but if you sit in Yukteswar's spot in the garden, then you get agitated, and all of that silt comes up. All that silt is like your issues, and Yukteswar starts clarifying them, and you start working them out. That's why we call Yukteswar the "no-nonsense" spot. So, I tell people to sit here for 10-15 minutes, get the information Yukteswar has for you, and then beeline it over to Mother's Pond to get a hug. Those are the ways you use these shrines.

It's been fun to give the Retreat Garden tours over the years. What I say about the lineage of our Master, I'm afraid, is not quite the official version. I paraphrase the official version something like this: At some unknown date in the distant past, Jesus came to Babaji and gave him the message, "My people are very good, and doing good works and everything, but they have forgotten how to have communion, inner communion with me. They are not talking to me."

Then Jesus asked, "Could you send somebody over to the West?" And Babaji answered, "Sure, I'll take care of that."

We know the next date in the story, 1861. Babaji called a disciple of his, Lahiri, and he said, "Lahiri, Jesus came to Babaji," etc., etc., etc. "and Jesus wanted Babaji to send someone to the West." And Lahiri said, "Sure, I'll take care of that."

A few decades later, Lahiri had a disciple, Sri Yukteswar, and he said, "Sri Yukteswar, Jesus came to Babaji, and Babaji came to me, and wanted us to send someone to the West who could teach people how to commune directly." What he's talking about is they need to bring the technique that will teach us how to do that.

Then it wasn't until 1920 that Yukteswar had a disciple named Paramhansa Yogananda who Yukteswar could tell the story to, and he told him, "And you're it, the one to go to teach the West!" We think things ought to happen in the blink of an eye. But this idea from the Divine took 100 years to come to fruition. And even at that, it was only the *beginning!*

So, this is the essence of what everyone needs to know about our lineage. I tell this story at the shrine for Lahiri in the Retreat Garden tours. Lahiri was a very inward person, and his spot is a very quiet, reflective spot.

Then I also tell the guests, "Whenever I decide to change anything in my life, I say it takes a minimum of 6 months. It's like turning the Queen Mary. You can't turn the Queen Mary like you can a speed boat. Most of the time, that's the way God works. And occasionally, it changes faster than that, but those are the times you don't want to be there!

The only way I can do these garden tour talks is if I have fun with them. I notice that when I start, so many of these city people just wonder, "*What* is going on? Why should I even *be* here?" They're thinking I'm going a little woo-woo. But by the end of the talk, they're all smiling.

Gurus of Self-Realization

I was a born teacher. That's why I talk all the time. It's not something I can help. I tell the youngsters over at the Retreat kitchen, "Because I do know how to do a lot of things, I'm going to tell you how to do something. I won't tell you *what* to do, but I will tell you *how* to do it. I am *driven* to tell you. On the other hand, I don't care what you do with that information. You can ignore it, you can change it, you can do whatever you want. But I have to say it. So just don't take it personally."

One time, after our team here at the Retreat read the article about me that had been included years before in the *Buckhorn Cookbook*, they started laughing. I asked them, "What's so funny?"

They all smiled shyly as one volunteered, "It says here that you give a lot of advice!"

MOTHER'S POND

At the Meditation Retreat somewhere around 2007, I got in an unusual mood for some reason. I just kept buying plants. But there was no area at that time being developed. I ended up keeping the newly bought plants over near the main entrance of the dining room, because that was the only place with a hose where I could keep them watered. The garden was nowhere as big as it is now, though it was more than big enough. I couldn't understand this passion for buying all these plants. It was like an obsession. This comes and goes, but why it was happening just then, I had no idea. There were even a few snide comments like, "Are you starting a *nursery* here?"

I wasn't told *not* to do any of this, explicitly. So, I just kept doing it. Somehow Nischala knew. This was not a normal phenomenon, and they seemed to sense that something special was happening here. And as much as they wanted me to stop—I could tell by different little conversations—they never actually told me to stop. And there were several reasons they could have done it. If I was going to use those plants, it would mean expanding where it would need more water and thus need more money. Here was another of the miracles in the garden—that the objections were kept down. Nakula was getting pressure from Atman Goering (Ananda Village manager) for me to stop, but Nakula never told me. Nor did Atman ever tell me directly. I would hear it mostly "through the grapevine." Besides, I was listening to *another* source. The only objection that I would constantly get, and still do, was about the water. And I would say, "You know, this is a cheap price to pay for all this. Your electric bill to run the water is less than my brother's domestic electric bill at his home in Florida." But in the end, I think it was mostly Divine Mother who must have tied Nakula's tongue and kept him from saying "No!" outright.

How Mother's Pond started is that I said to a group who were taking a retreat, "Someday there is going to be a pond over there." And one of the retreatants wrote out a check right then and there for the pond liner. Even with that, it still took over ten months before we got to it.

First, we needed to move the road that goes down to the cabins. That perimeter road used to go right in front of Joy Temple. That meant there was a road crossing where Mother's Pond is now. But that was the exact right spot for the new pond, even though I had to wait a long time for Nakula and his big backhoe to dig the hole.

Here's how Nischala tells what happened: "The road used to go right thru the middle. The temple here was a sacred space, already prayed in by many people for decades. But cars would race up, dust blowing everywhere, and the drivers would get out, slam their doors, then stride over to the temple. This road cutting thru the center of the Retreat grounds was breaking up the energy that was here. But Nakula is a builder, and when we first moved up to the Retreat, he had all these tractors."

(Charles again:) Back late in the year 2003, we decided we needed to rearrange all the roads uphill from where you pass the big wooden entrance sign welcoming you to the Meditation Retreat. People used to drive up the old roadway that's parallel and on the right of the current driveway. But that was the one that headed right through the garden. The two current main gates in the fence—on either side of the dining room—used to be joined together by an auto road in a straight line between them. But before we could dig the pond, we had to change all that. We ended up moving the perimeter road over a few hundred feet to allow the spot for this new pond.

Nischala continues, "After the road down the center of the Retreat disappeared, old-time Anandans would look a bit lost before asking, 'Where's the road?' Nakula had blocked it off. Nowadays, that old road is just a pebble path! I bow to Nakula. Because he has big energy, enough to take something like this garden on, when everyone else thought we were crazy. He's got the destiny, the will power, and the focus." Not to mention the *big* tractors!

(Charles once again:) Nakula and Nischala were very busy with the college, absorbed in all those issues. But one day he had the backhoe with him, and I asked if this might be a time he could do the new little pond. And he did. I had finally asked at just the right moment. Somehow, they recognized, as I always did, that this whole project was coming from a different source.

They *are* deep souls.

Now we were going to have to use the dirt from the pond's hole to finish and smooth the surrounding contours. What it took was this: Everybody else would go off to Sunday Service, and I would get on Nakula's tiny Bobcat tractor and try to figure out how to work it. Do you know how many levers there are in that thing? In addition, it doesn't help that I'm dyslexic. So, I'm sitting there scooping dirt, and moving it around. And at one point—I guess I had my foot on something I wasn't supposed to—the bucket kept lifting higher and higher until I dumped the whole load of dirt right on top of my head. It's for reasons like this that I would do the work in secret when everyone else was away—so they wouldn't see me embarrass myself!

Not only the roads, but we moved a lot of *paths*, too. I said to my old friend and co-worker Narada, "You know, we need to move this path."

And Narada replied, "We just recently did a lot of work putting that in."

And I said, "Ya, and we're gonna do a lot more work moving it! Because it's wrong!"

So, we moved it. And Narada looked at it, and said, "I didn't believe it. Just moving a few feet does make a difference. How did you know it was wrong, and the other one was going to be right?"

"It just felt wrong. It's an inner knowing—that there's not a *flow* the other way. Or sometimes because the path is *too* direct, making it a line lacking in aesthetics. It was just in the wrong place."

So anyway, getting back to my previous story, I had all these plants waiting for someplace to plant them, then bingo, bango, bongo, a landscaped pond came into existence.

We call the pond that finally came into existence—the one with statutes of Jesus and Mary—Mother's Pond. We call it that because when we were working on it, everybody felt very nurtured there—blessed even—like being hugged by Divine Mother. The energy there is very loving—*unconditional* love. It continues to have that feeling to this day.

Nakula Cryer on his tractor

Mary and her son Jesus at Mother's Pond

Mother's Pond

Sunlight illuminating the oak trees

New baby for the garden

A riot of colors

Counseling session

THE WELL, THE PRAYER, AND THE GUSHER

Just after putting lots of this new garden in, our well went dry. It went down to three or four gallons a minute, and it was sludge. We were in terrible trouble, because it was hot, and even if I watered the garden only minimally, the retreatants still needed water for drinking and bathing. We were trucking water up the hill and trying to fill our water tank. We needed a new well. First, we hired a dowser and a geologist to come out, and they both picked the same spot. So that's what we told the drilling company: "Drill here."

And they drilled, and they drilled, and they drilled, and they drilled. And there was no water. We could only go down to 600 feet and still be able to pump the water up. At 590, all the big wigs gathered with sad faces because we'd just wasted $10,000 dollars digging a dry hole. I prayed a desperate demand to Divine Mother: "We've been following *Your* guidance. WHY DID YOU HAVE US PUT THIS GARDEN IN, IF YOU WEREN'T GOING TO GIVE US ENOUGH WATER? You did it for Moses. You did it for Lourdes. COULDN'T YOU PLEASE DO IT FOR US?" And at 596 we hit a gusher! 40 gallons per minute, which is very unusual for this area. Not only that, but it pushed half-way up the pipe on its own, so we only have to use electricity to pump from 350 feet. It hasn't even varied during this latest drought. There sure is Something watching out for all of us.

It goes with the affirmation we so often use up here, "Lord, give us what we need at the time we need it." We don't ask for a lot. It takes total trust to step forward blindly, and that's basically what we've been doing up here at the Retreat, and at the garden, and with Ananda. We just keep following the guidance and putting one foot in front of the other. And just when it seems like we're about to step off the edge of a cliff—you know, like running out of water—then, suddenly, we get an abundant supply!

It would have been harder to run this place on that old well. And it didn't make any sense to any of us, especially to Nakula, why I kept putting in more garden, since we didn't have enough water to run the one that we had. But I had to follow the guidance. I was being guided to do this.

Nischala added these thoughts about this period at the Meditation Retreat:

"I think the garden had become Charles' salvation. This was really his dharma. Nakula and I got busy with the college. And the college students needed something to do. So, they worked in the garden with Charles. We made it part of their karma yoga. Charles was always having them do things. Charles would just come up with projects, like the little pond nearest to the Bungalows that they call Mother's Pond. They built the greenhouse. They built the raised beds. They built the chicken enclosure. Then the students, under Pablo's guidance, built that little hand-built temple that today we call the Temple of Joy.

"When we first started out, everything was little. The plants all started tiny. Charles would remind us, 'Someday they'll be big!' Ananda held all its Sevaka Retreats up here. During one of those, I remember looking from the dining room to the temple, and all the trees and garden things that Charles had done were just beautiful. It was like, 'Oh my God, it's actually happening.' There were flowering dogwoods, bearded iris, Japanese maples—a whole variety of things.

"During another of those Sevaka Retreats, Swamiji was with us, and we were having lunch outside on the picnic tables. Nearby, Charles had planted some strawberries. And Swami looked down, and said, 'Oh my God, strawberries at the Meditation Retreat? I never would have imagined!'"

SWAMI ADDS HIS BLESSINGS

On the path leading to the temple, behind the biggest statue of Mother Mary, there is an area dedicated to Swami Kriyananda. In June of 2009, I was at Sunday Service, and during the Story of the Fledgling Bird (part of Sunday morning's Festival of Light at Ananda), I often tend to drift without focusing on it, without thinking about anything else particularly. Then all of a sudden, I always seem to come back exactly at the sentence that I'm supposed to hear.

But this one day—the best way I can describe it is this—there was this thought that passed in front of me like a wave—almost visual, but there was no *thing* there. There was this gentle wave going through, and as it passed, it spoke. It said, "Perhaps it's time for a shrine for Swami." I instantly *knew* it was true guidance. I didn't even question it. And I said, in my head, "Well, where would I put that? It's not *easy* to find shrine spots!" And instantly I had a vision of the spot, and what it would look like. Then suddenly, I'm back in the Temple listening to the Bird Story.

When I got home to the Retreat, I walked over to the place the vision had shown, and it was an area where there had been no intention of having anything happen. I walked over to it, stood there, and got real quiet. My feelers were out. I thought, "There's something going on here." And it started to turn me, clockwise. You know if you let everything else go—just release it—you'll go with the flow. As I'm going around, I keep my eyes straight ahead, and I realize, "The trees are growing in a *circle* here." And I think, "Oh, wow!" We had discovered a vortex. Talented psychics can see a shimmering along the edge of this spot.

From the very beginning, and without knowing what the psychics saw, I had said, "It's bringing energy in." The Lahiri Mandir over at the Expanding Light goes the other way, counterclockwise. But this one at the Retreat is an energy vortex that's spinning clockwise, drawing energy in. On one of the tours, I told the group, "You know, this spot is bringing energy in. I would expect that this might be an interesting place to sit to commune with the astral world and the other side." And this woman standing just behind me says, "Oh, I was here yesterday, and all my deceased relatives were standing around." This kind of thing has started happening here more and more.

If you want to reach out to the universe, you go to spots like Lahiri Mandir. But if you want wisdom, if you want to talk to Swami, or to any other souls in the higher planes, the right spot is where the energy is coming in, like at this shrine for Swami here at the Meditation Retreat.

Now there was another part of that vision, besides showing me that space. In the vision, the space was round, and it looked pretty much like it does now, but there was a structure in the middle. That structure hasn't yet come into manifestation, because in the vision it was fuzzy. I remember smiling, "I don't have to do that part ... *yet*!" I've learned to put "yet" on such thoughts. Because I also never thought I had to do the garden around Grandmother tree, either, but later I had to. My vision showed me a bit of what the structure was to look like. It had columns; it was white. Looked like something you would see at an Indian cemetery. "Lotusy" top, or domed top. It was fuzzy, but maybe five columns in a circle. It's like a monument, or a memorial feeling to it. There's something in the middle. We have some of Swami's hair there now. We did that to help strengthen the vibration that was already there.

At one of the retreats that we hosted for the Village residents, we told Swami about the vortex, and that it was dedicated to him, and asked him if he might bless it. Swami went over, sat in the spot for about 15 minutes, and blessed it.

Unlike many disciples at Ananda, I usually tended *not* to add the honorific "ji" to the end of Swami's name. You know, in the beginning, I didn't like Swami *that* much. Nowadays if I saw him, I would call him Swamiji. I had gotten to that point long before he passed. The final healing was when, in 2006, I was in Gurgaon, India, and all the people from the ashram went to some party at an Indian devotee's home. All the Westerners were gathered around Swamiji in the living room, and I'm sitting there looking at him, and just *knew* what I was seeing. I was looking at a *saint*. He was glowing! Swami still had a thread of humanness, sure, but he was beyond. You *know* when you're in that kind of pure presence. Before that, all I could see was his attachments. But when I looked at him this time, there was only that one thin, thin, *thin* attachment. I don't know where I get the audacity to say such things. It's just these inner knowings that show up.

I've always known that this garden was dedicated to Swami. When that voice said, way back in 1994, "I said *six* feet! This is going to be a place of pilgrimage." Subliminally, in my head, I remember thinking, "A pilgrimage for *what*?" The answer came, "For Swami."

The time I got that wave of a whisper that it was time for a shrine to Swami was almost the exact same day, June 6, 2009, and time that Swami lay close to death over in Italy. Some didn't expect him to survive another day. None of us knew this until later. Asha (who co-founded Ananda Palo Alto and teaches worldwide as one of Swamiji's "Global Ambassadors") was sitting by a couch at his home in Assisi where Swami lay in deep stillness. She feared he might have already left the body. Then, suddenly he sat up with renewed strength and immediately began to dictate the book that started the Nayaswami Order, *A Renunciate Order for the New Age*. Soon afterwards, Swami told Asha that the satanic forces had been trying to prevent this very movement from being brought into the world.

2010s

SWAMI'S HOUSE

In 2010, Biraj invited me over to India to help landscape around Swamiji's new house on Ananda's land outside Pune. I thought I was going over to plant a few trees. But when I got to the site, it was a *huge* canvas to landscape! Heaps of rubble were everywhere. And 150 Indians running around. And Jaya Helin (now co-Spiritual Director of Ananda India) and Vidura Smallen had dug huge trenches everywhere to install all the plumbing and sewage pipes Swami's house needed. I said, "Oh my God, what have I gotten myself into?"

Biraj tried to apologize. He said, "I swear I had this area completely cleared for you the day before yesterday." And he *had*.

I said to myself, "I've got to take a walk." And I prayed real hard, saying, "You have to show me how to do this. This is more than I can deal with." I realized that before I could plant any plants, I was going to have to build walls for terracing the hillside. And I came back, stood atop the tallest mound of rubble, and prayed, "Ya know, You need to show me the lines." We couldn't even see the ground due to all the rubble scattered around. Then suddenly, but very faintly, the lines started to appear. And I was sort of tracing them with my finger, so I'd remember where they were. And I looked up, and all the Indian workers had stopped. They were watching me intently, no doubt thinking, "*What's* he doing?" The magician had arrived! From then on it was easy. The hard part was the *seeing*. After that, it was just getting those Indian laborers to do this project differently than they had done for the past five thousand years of their civilization!

I remember the second garden retaining wall that we put up following those lines that I'd been shown. For some reason, I walked away and let the local workmen finish it. When I got back, well, I had let them have a try, but ... it was like, "What on earth have you done? That's not what I asked you to do. Does *this* look like *that?*" pointing to the wall I had finished previously as their model. They had just reverted to how they had always done things.

Biraj, Jaya, Wyatt & Vidura atop Charles' garden walls at Swami's home in Pune

It got particularly difficult when I had two different crews, one from the nearby village, and the other hired from the big city in Pune. I would have to go down there and work with that other group a bit. It would have been easier to just work with the villagers, especially if we had only been building concrete walls—they would have known what to do for that. But here we were laying walls made from rocks. Previously, they had built the retaining wall down by the kitchen building, and that one had collapsed. I wasn't involved with that one. I made them do big rocks first, for the foundation at the bottom. I got the big tractor to place the big ones, and they were so pleased that I had gotten that help. Then we had to get the stonecutters to cut some of the rocks. I liked that wall, sloping at an angle like that. I was glad I had left by the time they built the big thick wall below the *kutirs* (small, simple residences.) That came out so industrial. It didn't have anything like the same vibration as the ones we had built together.

The guy in charge of the workers came up and asked me where to put the wall below the patio. I told him, "Just make it curvy. No straight lines!"

I remember that time when the ABC thing, or VCR, or JCB—the thing like a Caterpillar-brand tractor—was there. Two days before, this hillside had been pristine. I witnessed it happen many times. Then here is this big machine with its huge metal claws, and it was getting ready to take down one of the acacia trees that was going to be what was left of the natural landscaping. I remember racing madly across the cluttered ground and jumping up onto this tractor and pounding on it. I won, too! I got him to leave the acacia be. Two seconds later, that tree would have been history. All these local people were standing around looking on, and thinking, "*What's* he doing? Why's he doing *that?* That would have been more firewood for us!" Ananda bought that land from them, but those locals didn't lose anything. They kept coming and cutting down any of the trees they wanted for firewood. They had been doing that for centuries. They thought, "Why stop now?"

Building those garden walls for Swami's home in Pune was quite an experience!

Kriyananda in 1970's

Swamiji in 2010

After all that intense work with Swami's Pune house, Mary Mintey (who for years ran a beautiful boutique for Ananda Assisi) and I spent 10 days at Lake Pushkar in India. Then I hightailed it to Lakshman Jula, just upstream from Rishikesh. I loved that place. Got a room in the big Seva Ashram, right on the Ganges. They had big, nice rooms, as well as not-so-nice cheaper rooms. I ended up with a big room right on the Ganges. Then I moved across the river to the Oasis, the German Bakery hotel. There I had a room right on the town plaza. It was *Kumbha Mela* time (the massive religious festival that happens in India every 3 years) taking place that year just down river in Haridwar, but they still do all that pilgrimage stuff even there in Lakshman Jula. And I was sitting there, watching these groups of Indians going into all the temples, and ringing all the bells. Whole villages come with all their utensils hanging off the poles they balance on their shoulders.

While in Lakshman Jula, I realized my head was not in a good space and had not been for some time. I didn't know what to do. I was getting depressed. Nothing was working. That's a very unusual feeling for me. I knew I needed to let go of something. I was praying, "Tell me what it is I'm supposed to let *go* of, I will be glad to let it go." Out the window, I was watching one of the Indian's donkeys getting all loaded up, and it was time to go, but the donkey wouldn't go. And I said, "That's just like me. Stubborn jackass!"

I came back to the States, but I was still depressed. I couldn't figure out what to do. I was in kind of a dark mood. I just couldn't figure out what it was I was supposed to let go of. And I crawled out of bed one morning. I rolled over to my little altar, and I looked at Master's (Yogananda) picture and said, "Sir, I'm giving this *all* to you!" You know, I got so light, I felt like I had come off my cushion. I felt like I was filled with helium. "You know", I said to Yogananda, "You could have said '*all*'. You could have *said* I needed to let go of everything!"

Even to this day, I have to be vigilant. It's attachments to likes and dislikes, preferences. Nothing big. Little teeny things. I had already let go of all the big stuff years before. Sometimes I remind Master: "I give you my whole life—You have *all* of me—therefore, I expect to be taken care of completely." And I am. Here I am officially indigent, and yet I'm living like a prince. I do live very simply. There's only a $10 phone bill every month, and a $21 TV bill. I wouldn't even need a car, except that I'm responsible for two town trips each week of supplies for the Meditation Retreat.

DURGA AND VIDURA

For a while, we had Chaitanya Mahoney (who now serves at Ananda Sacramento) as manager for the Retreat. And during that time, Durga brought a group and led them on a walk through the gardens. And I said to her, "You know, we're looking for a Spiritual Director up here, and you would be perfect." It still took a while ... a year and a half later to be exact.

Durga and Vidura Smallen weren't scheduled to be here at all. After Chaitanya, it had become a ship without a captain. Raghu Clark was hoping to fill the job next, and had already been announced to begin, so in July 2013 just as a stopgap Durga and Vidura Smallen agreed to come up here "for three months" while waiting for the new leaders to arrive. At the eleventh hour, it didn't work out for Raghu, so Durga and Vidura were asked if they would be willing to lead the Retreat "for three more months." After that, no one ever asked again if they'd be willing—it simply became theirs to do. Perhaps it wasn't the Smallen's first choice at the beginning, but later on you'd have had to pry the Meditation Retreat away from them. They loved it, even though it sure was a lot of work. During their time here, they totally reinvented the Meditation Retreat.

You know how the first garden tours began? Durga and Vidura had been here at the Retreat almost a year. In spring of 2014 Durga hosted one of her famous teas. But this time she invited the whole of Ananda Village up for tea. We had events happening, and tours of all the new indoor spaces. It was quite an event. They had me give a talk about the garden. They both recognized what was happening. Vidura introduced me. 60-80 people took the tour. Up until then, I just hadn't put it all into a cohesive presentation. I was shy about it because it sounded like too much bragging. "I, I, I." I didn't feel right to talk about myself so much. Except that for a while I did happen to be the channel for what was taking place, through me. When you get visions and hear things, you're foolish if you don't respond. But when that sweet voice originally said, "You've come to finish the landscaping," it didn't make any sense to me.

Durga and Vidura Smallen, Retreat managers

I have a hard time bossing people. I'm really good at telling people the next thing that could be done, but not good at bossing them. I'll explain it to them. Then if they do it or not, that's up to them. A bit like what Swamiji wrote about in *The Art of Supportive Leadership*. A lot of leaders annoy people who work under them because they're used to telling people what they must do. And that's *not* supportive leadership. Those kinds of people get themselves in trouble, especially here at Ananda. It takes more time to do it right. Many of us leaders get too impatient, partly because we realize how short the time is that we must do all this. Rather than the Ananda principle of "People are more important than things," we too often put projects before people. I work hard *not* to do that—but I don't always get it right.

Women's retreat

Paramhansa Yogananda

Sign for Ananda's Meditation Retreat

Durga's cookies

Charles, Brannon Forrester & Vidura--a good team

Vidura is excellent at maintaining the right balance in this. He is so good at getting people to work and at keeping them motivated. I have trouble telling people, “It’s time to get up now. You’ve been sitting there long enough. Now get to work. Biraj had the following experience of Vidura’s powers of motivation. ”It was amazing years ago to do a ride-along with him. I asked if I could hang out and chat with him for a morning. And he said, ‘Sure, come on.’ I arranged this event days ahead of time. And when the day finally came, I showed up, and Vidura said, ‘OK, jump in. We’ve got some things to do.’ I think he did this deliberately to help teach me how to be an effective leader. That truck zipped along back and forth all over Ananda Village. He had about seven people each doing different projects. And *his* only job, apparently, was to be sure they had the paintbrush or this or that they needed to do their job, then to just give them a little nudge of energy and encouragement they needed and drive away. Vidura was an excellent foreman. He kept seven projects going at once! It was a great lesson for me about true supportive leadership.”

(Charles again:) Vidura knows how to get other people to do it. He knows how to get it done. What he's done at the Retreat is amazing; it's astounding. Of course, he was the general manager for *all* of Ananda Village for many years—over a decade. He has a proven record of success at managing and working with people.

But he can drive you crazy because he's ultra-spontaneous. If he sees something he doesn't resonate with, rather than try to understand it and fix it, he gets rid of it. He's always getting rid of all the potentially useful "bones" in our junk piles. A chair with a broken slat, rather than try to fix it, he throws it out.

About these little things, they just think *I'm* crazy. But we work things out. The Retreat managers let me work my creative side sometimes, especially if it saves the Retreat money. For instance, the two sheds I use for my hand tools and for my shovels—one used to be the cedarpaneled sauna for Devotion Cabin (what we used to call the old Sacramento house), and the other used to be Devotion's former outhouse. They let me move both of those to the far end of the dining room as storage for my garden stuff.

Mother Mary along the path

Lupines surrounding Yukteshwar's Shrine

Lahiri Shrine

I had to build my own kitchen onto Renunciation cabin, because the Retreat had a cook who kept putting chilis in everything. I couldn't eat that stuff! I was working 10-12 hours every day to get the job done. I even got as creative as running a water hose from Swami's Dome to supply my cabin with running water!

Master is taking care of us. I told Durga and Vidura that they shouldn't worry. As soon as we start worrying, as long as we hold on to even one thread, and figure we have to start doing it, the powers that be—Master and all—will stand back and say, "OK, *you* go for it." But, if we totally let it go, we'll have abundance.

GRANDMOTHER TREE

Doing this garden has made me feel more connected to Divine Mother. I see God all through this hilltop up here, and especially in the creations of this garden. It's surely not coming from me – it's just coming *through* me. If I'm not connected, then I won't know *what* I'm doing, or what to do. I would just stumble around.

On the opposite side of the garden from Grandfather is another ancient oak. There was nothing surrounding it but leaves and weeds. We had no intention at all, except that every time I looked in that direction, I thought it looked sort of "Japanesey." It seemed Oriental. The paths that are there now are all the original ones. I didn't put those paths in. The only path I put in was the one actually stepping up to Grandmother tree. So, people had walked that way a lot. After we had found Grandfather, we started calling that other big tree Grandmother. I took tours through, and we would bushwhack over through the leaves, and I would tell them that someday there was going to be a garden here. And this one group asked, "What's holding it up?"

The first thought in my head was "Well, I don't really *want* to do it!" But then my mind said, "I can't tell these people that. I have a reputation here to uphold." So, I had to think of reasons. Then I answered, "I wouldn't even think of starting something like this without the watering system. The controls for that alone are $1000! So, we haven't even thought about it." When they left three days later, they handed me a check for that very amount. And it went from there.

First, I put a bench near Grandmother, and I sat down and got quiet. Once I sat down and looked at that tree, it looked different than when I had been looking at that tree from a standing position. I realized what a force field I was in. And again, my favorite reaction came out: "Wow!" You know, there was something going on there. I'm not nosey, and I don't need to know all the little details. Someone else can do that. But then this tree spoke to me, and I hear, "Yes, Grandmother—like Golda Meir, the Grandmother of Israel." I was stunned! One tough lady, but one who was also very compassionate. Strong, yet loving energy. The tree did NOT say, "Margaret Thatcher." That would have been a big difference. Very loving, but at the same time strong and powerful. Golda was part of the birthing of Israel, but also, I believe, one of the sanest leaders they ever had. Immediately after that, people started having awarenesses while sitting under Grandmother Tree. That's become one of the favorite spots in the whole garden. They sit there, and they get Grandmother. But you have to still the part of you that's going to rot—meaning your brain—and listen with your heart.

Quince overlooking Babaji Pond

Grandmother Tree

Quan Yin at the base of Grandmother Tree

After I had received guidance that this should happen around Grandmother, I just started buying plants. I had no idea where exactly I was going to put each of them. But I know the area well. I know what kinds of plants to put in deep shade. Other places would get spotted with sunlight. So those things I know. Whenever I would go to town I would go to the nursery and walk through. Things would just catch my eye. It's like the proverbial story about the book you need that drops off the shelf onto you. The plants do that to me. And I just buy them when they do.

So, I bought all these plants, but then I got really sick! I was barely able to keep hand watering the containers. Two guys arrived right then who knew how to plant. I showed them what I would do for planting the first pot, but after that they did the rest.

Angel in bloom

There was a fun experience. A left-brained accountant came for a stay at the Retreat and volunteered to do the very linear task of laying out the watering system. I asked him to prepare himself by reading *The Findhorn Garden* book. In the beginning I had to tell him exactly what to do. He kept asking me, "How many drippers?" And I'd tell him. But after a while, I began responding simply, "Ask the plant!" The reason we can't hear nature is we *think* we can't. Just like the famous old children's story of *The Little Engine that Could*. Think you can, and you can. So he would keep asking me how many drippers. And I kept telling him to ask the plant. And I would come along afterwards and make the correction. But it wasn't long before I didn't have to make any corrections whatsoever. He just had it. He still didn't know one plant variety from another, but he was talking to them, and he was tuning in. If I can do it, and *he* can do it, *you* can do it too. "I think I can, I think I can."

INTUITION

In 2017, I thought I would be moving up to Laurelwood near the Ananda Portland Center. I had taken my soulmate Ruth up to Ananda House—it was time for her to receive more supportive care—and when I got back to the Meditation Retreat, I heard inside, "Yes, Go. Yes, Stay." I was sitting here, thinking like a song that was playing through my head, "Should I stay, or should I go?" I kept meditating, and my head kept spinning with, "Should I stay, or should I go?" I had already picked out my room at the Laurelwood campus. I had written down all the dimensions, and I was picking out the furniture that I would take, and what I would do. But I didn't know if I should do it. So, I made an appointment with Devi.

I'd told her my dilemma before I went. And she meditated on this. When I arrived to see Devi, she admitted it was very confusing. She had been getting "You need to stay here, but you need to go there." Pretty much the same thing I was getting. Thanks a lot! So, we talked for about half an hour. Devi and I have an interesting connection. And we came up with this: I need to stay here—she said my soul is rooted at the Meditation Retreat—but I need to go consult there. So, it ended up meaning, "Stay here, but go there when needed."

What this garden does never ceases to amaze me. I'm somewhat disconnected from it. Sometimes, I wonder if I'm just making this all up. Compared to what people consider normal, the guidance I receive never seems real. We've all been taught that this is not possible. I mean, if you hear voices, you're supposed to go see a shrink. You get these thoughts, and you get labeled "a problem"—that there's something mentally wrong. But when I get these things, I don't have a choice. Nobody in their right mind would do this! But it takes that kind of surrender to it, and just knowing.

That's why Biraj wanted to write this book about me. Because just like in the other book he wrote recently, I, too, have a way that intuition comes to me. It's like being a living example of one way that intuition can manifest. These things just *come* to me. They don't come through any willpower of my own. I truly don't know how I've done this life. Because *I* haven't. That's how Swami, too, used to put it: "I didn't write any of these books," he would say. The Divine did it through him. It's the hardest thing to prove. If you asked me—my rational mind—to do some of these things, I would freak out. When they asked me to landscape the temple, three different times I said, "No way!" Because *I* didn't know how to do it. But Someone did, because then I saw the lines, and I just surrendered totally. I think *that's* the trick. It doesn't work until you surrender. You must surrender the ego that says, "I know how to do this," or "First, I need to know how to do that." No, you just have to surrender, and except.

My story about how the Sri Yukteswar shrine came about is all about surrendering the ego and accepting the guidance. I tested Divine Mother, to see if she *would* put a hundred-dollar bill in the palm of my hand. We do have to be careful that it's not coming from ego. So, just to be sure, I test often!

I'm starting to understand the process a little more. People's intuition comes in several different forms. Some people see. Some people hear. It comes through the senses for many. But most of mine are just a knowing. It comes from a place that you just *know* is correct. It's a knowing that is just different than the normal thoughts.

It smells different. It *tastes* different. It *feels* different. These trigger you to pay attention to that thought. Once you identify it, you *know*. Once you discern *this* knowing is right, and *that* other one just isn't, you *know*. It all comes clear from experimentation. I can't remember exactly when I did that experimenting, but I did it early on.

After a while with this sense of knowing, it just becomes second nature. You know when you're in that flow, and you know when you're not. When you're in that flow, it's like being on the paved road. It flows. It might be hilly, sure. But it's not the same as having all the bumps on Jackass Flat Road on the way to the Meditation Retreat. When you start feeling like that, it's time to start saying, "Whoa!" You can have obstructions and things on the smooth highway, but you don't get that rattle. I tell my people on the garden tours, "If you're going to San Francisco, do you want to go on the paved road, or do you want to go on the dirt and gravel road? When you choose to ignore guidance, it's the dirt and gravel road you've chosen!"

That sense of guidance, like when it told me it was time for a shrine for Swami, has a great sense of peace that comes with the guidance. That little extra sensation that comes to remind you this is something true and special. After you pay attention to that a little bit, then you catch it all the time.

I once was asked by a very high soul, "Is your intuition fallible, or infallible?" I had to sit and think, and what came was, "Well, when it pertains to me, it's infallible. But when it pertains to anything outside of me, it is definitely fallible." When it's something I need to do, it's infallible. It's a must. It's not really a choice when that happens. But if I get an awareness about you, that's not so infallible.

See, I'm only a little bit psychic. There are people who are *hugely* psychic. I can't get the guidance on command. I must wait until it comes. Nowadays, I always wait until I get guidance to do most anything. It could turn out to be incorrect, but I've trained myself to respond to these inner stirrings, no matter what the brain in my head thinks. That happened with this garden. I would not have done this if I had gotten a vision of this entire garden ahead of time, no way! I would have run somewhere else, quick. But Mother and Master knew to feed me just little pieces at a time, otherwise I would have gotten scared. It's like when I was six or seven years into the spiritual journey, investigating this and that. I remember saying, "If I had known it was going to take this long, I don't think I ever would have started." But by this time, I'm too far into it to quit. Same with this garden!

Sometimes I do hear audibly, but more often it's an inside knowing. And sometimes I do see the lines, like what I was doing for Swami's house in Pune. I was praying hard; I needed to be able to tell where anything was—it had been like picking your way through a junk yard.

We all need to get out of being in the left-brain so much and get more into the right-brain. The left-brain will too often take you down the wrong path. But you can't throw it out. You *do* need the left-brain in order to operate in this world.

For a while, I took a vacation from kriya. I did some with the group while I was up in Laurelwood. But more often I just sit. I have more of a communing meditation lately. To me meditation is when you sit down and calm yourself, and then you can feel, and talk with, God. That's the goal of every kind of meditation. So I just do that all the time. I got on to that when I wasn't doing the formal techniques for a while, and you know that you're not meditating formally, so therefore your whole day has to be a meditation. So, I would do that. Like, "God, I'm going to pick up this napkin." I would just talk to God all the time, whatever I was doing.

Mostly, I'm talking to God about nature, like, "Look at that tree." Or the negative things, too, like, "Look what that idiot's doing!" Sometimes, when I've been a little naughty, I just say, "Ya know, Sir, I hope you just enjoyed that as much as I did!" You can't exclude God and Guru from anything. To me, guru is God. The whole point of the spiritual path is to connect with God. When you are connecting with God, the day-to-day actions we did when we started on the spiritual path are less crucial because the Goal has been achieved. Finally, we're constantly doing what the Goal helped us realize was possible.

After a while *that* becomes the sadhana, and I don't have to consciously talk to God, I'm just "there." Some people get breakthroughs doing kriya, but for me that's a challenge. It's a bit of a chore, like going to the gym! Occasionally I can get into an easy rhythm with it. But the other way gives me pleasure, and comfort, and wisdom, and knowledge. We each use the means that work for us. More often, I just say to Guru, "I'm with You all the time."

Master says, "Think Me near, and I will be near." I figure that's what I'm doing. And He always is. I was told early on in my spiritual quest, "Charles, if you're praying to God, you're praying too far." We at Ananda pray to God in form as Yogananda. Yogananda and all the saints become the physical expression of God for us. Yogananda and the saints definitely were a part of God, and they were much more connected than most of the rest of us. They were *aware* that they're part of God, while we're most often merely affirming it.

You must be sure you're using the tools of the path enough so that you really *can* make connection with the Divine. However, once you make connection with the Divine, and you're keeping that connection, don't worry about the little stuff. It's important to have done enough kriya—to build up the electromagnetic conductor in your spine—so that we can handle the intensity of contact with the Divine, so that we can stay with God. Yogananda came over to teach us Americans how to commune directly with the Divine. By channeling the energy up and down our spines during kriya, we widen our spiritual passageway, so that the energy won't scorch us in our efforts to connect with God.

Once in a while it's really special. But most of the time it's just like when I'm talking to you with a knowing. Most of the time it's just that I say something, and I know what God is answering. Like if I talk to you, or to Devi, and I needed advice that I knew you could give; all I'd have to do is think of you and I would get your advice, though it might not be what I *wanted* to hear!

Often the response is very different than what I would have told myself. It shocks me sometimes. Like that man who asked me, "Where are you going?" when I was ready to leave Florida, and I wanted to go to the Southwest. And I swear it was like one of those cartoons where the light bulb goes on and all of a sudden it says in a funny little, high-pitched voice, "Oregon."

So, I had to answer the man, "Guess I'm going to Oregon."

As when I received the guidance to return to the Meditation Retreat the second time, sometimes it takes a while once you receive the guidance, to follow it. You must move it from where you received it in the right brain over into the left brain. I was trying to squeeze things into the left brain, and I'm sitting having a nice meditation. Suddenly, I hear another funny little, high-pitched voice say, "Assisi." I knew exactly what it meant. And I cry out in exasperation, "But that's in *Europe!*" Then I knew I had to go to Assisi *before* I came back to the Meditation Retreat. Then I asked, "How long?" I heard, "Six months!" Only *then* would I be allowed to return home to the Meditation Retreat.

When I was about to head out for Ananda Assisi, I sent a long, pleading letter ahead of time explaining why I could *not* work in a kitchen. Nonetheless, I ended up for six months in their kitchen. And it helped me get beyond some of that burn-out that I had experienced in the U.N. Plaza Hotel's kitchen. Just goes to show, you get exactly what you need, rather than what you want. At least the Italians, unlike the East Indians, don't eat too many chilis!

Actually, I started to work off that old kitchen burn-out when I was at Buckhorn, when they needed a breakfast cook. Since I'd never been on breakfast at the U.N. Plaza, I thought I could probably do that. And it worked. Prior to that, for a whole seven years, I couldn't even stand to boil water.

If it had been up to me, I would have stayed in Italy forever. They served pasta every day, which I loved. Even today, if someone were to ask me what kind of restaurant I would like to go to, it would be Italian. The Italians smother everything in so much olive oil. They are so heart healthy. Also, they eat bitter greens, really bitter ones like wild dandelions. But they showed me how to cook them, and I even came to like them.

Aum, the vibration underlying all creation

Master's bust by Gary Roller

The pollinators

Back in the 1980's when I asked myself what was the most ludicrous thing I could do—the answer was go around the world—India popped into my head. So that's where I went. At the time, I had no idea that Master had been there all along whispering his guidance to me.

I think I live my life ahead of myself, and then explain what just happened. I never know what I'm doing, even while I'm doing it. I realized early in life that I'm an opportunist, I watch for opportunities to show themselves. I don't plan ahead. I can't even tell you, "Let's have lunch." I watch for opportunities, and that's what's allowed me to experience so many lives in this one lifetime. It's because I've stayed flexible. Since being at Ananda, I've learned to embrace it to a fuller extent. Going with the flow and realizing it's all a blessing. I wouldn't change a thing. Now as to my physical needs I would change a lot of things. But my spiritual needs, I wouldn't change a thing! No question, it's been an interesting life!

COOPERATING WITH THE NATURE SPIRITS

Have you heard of Findhorn? That's the place in Scotland where the nature spirits agreed to work with humankind big time. The Findhorn gardeners learned to meditate and listen to the nature spirits. I was trained in Findhorn's methods back in 1980 at that Sirius Community in Massachusetts. People often ask how this garden at our Retreat is different from Findhorn's. Actually, this garden is not a lot different. Findhorn's garden is famous because it's built in an impossible place. It's built next to the sea, with the winds and the salt winds buffeting it, and the soil is all sand! It's not conducive to a garden. And yet a magnificent garden has grown up there.

This hilltop at the Meditation Retreat is a dry hilltop—it's one-degree away from being a desert. So, it's not conducive to gardening either. Yet this garden, too, is flourishing. Things are growing much better here than they would have even in an environment more friendly to the plants. That's because the nature spirits, both here and at Findhorn, have agreed this is a worthwhile project and are happy with it. The nature spirits have joined forces with our effort to produce this. It would not thrive as much as it has, and be as beautiful as it is, without their cooperation.

I think this garden came about to help uplift people's spirits and to connect them more with the Divine. It gives them a place to sit and meditate, and to feel the presence of Divine Mother. Beauty opens the heart. You can feel the nature spirits in this garden. They're much more active than if you went to a garden in town or in the cities. They're much more present here;

they're more accessible. The nature spirits normally don't expose themselves that much to man because man's vibration can be a little disruptive to them. But up here, because we're meditators, they're much more comfortable... and come out more towards the surface.

Me amidst the Black Eye Susans

Yellow and rust iris

Bearded peach-colored iris

When the garden was nowhere near as big as it is now—it was mostly around the Babaji pond—there was nothing much anywhere else at that time. And one day I was walking across that planted area, walking from my home in Renunciation Cabin to take a shower in the Bathhouse, and I went into bliss. Full blown, tears streaming down, and with that sweetness! In that state, there's just nothing else; everything outward literally disappears from our consciousness.

"Why?" I asked. Well, after a week-long group Kriya Retreat, this was a day they were doing a kriya initiation up in the Meditation Retreat Temple. All week everybody had been in silence and in deep meditation. And when I walked out the other side of that planted area, abruptly it all came right back to normal. So, I turned around to go back through the garden to check it out. And I went right back into that full-blown bliss. Every time I would walk across the garden that day, I would go into bliss. So, I tried to walk across it a lot! I would get that blissful grin on my face, and tears would just start streaming from my eyes—just in bliss. When you are in that state, there's nothing else. Everything else just disappears from our awareness. But after two or three times, I realized that it wasn't me that was instigating this bliss, it was the garden that was in bliss. The devas were in bliss. They were so thrilled and excited that this sacred ceremony was happening, and that they were part of it. It just brought that joy in and created bliss. So, the garden can be in bliss, too, when it's used in that fashion.

Swami found us a good place!

About the time that we started doing this garden, we started feeding the birds. And we always had a few birds up here, but never a lot. And now we have all kinds of birds that are always around and singing and hopping around and eating and drinking water. I've noticed that it brings a special delight to people. There's something about birds—maybe that they can fly, or that they can soar—that possibly helps us soar. It's been mentioned a lot by people that the birds here have brought them great joy. And if they are experiencing joy from seeing the birds, they're moving that much closer to Divine Mother, and to the joy that we receive in bliss. Bliss is merely one more step beyond joy!

Just by sitting in the garden people attune to the nature spirits. It affects people even if they don't know what's happening. It's the same as when people walk into a room and the room is in order—they're affected by it, but they don't necessarily know why.

Yogananda said that it's easier to see God in nature than in any other way, and this garden is filled with nature. It's a little different than Crystal Hermitage's Garden at Ananda Village that is a more formal garden. You can see God in the gorgeous beauty of that nature. Up here, this garden is more natural in its feel, and over time will become even more so.

I do the watering as a meditation, as service, as communing, as talking to the plants, listening, and being in wonder that all of this is taking place. Each day when I'm watering these plants is the time when I'm really communing with them. I tend to do hand watering for several years with each new planting area. The area around the big path coming in from the main entrance gate is on automatic sprinklers, but I'm watering the edges. There are still a lot of corrections that need to be done to these watering systems that I just haven't had time to do. (I need a left-brain type to come in.) So, I'm watering, and I'm seeing how they're doing. Is there a little problem here? Are their roots reaching out right? Things like that.

This is a meditation garden, and I notice that when I see people using the garden, they tend to come to a kind of peace and often awe—awe of this garden. But this garden *is* Divine Mother's, so it connects people with *Her*.

Before, when it was just raw manzanita up here, people didn't tend to linger. They came and took care of their business, then left. It was very, very yang—masculine, mental, harsh. What we've done is added the yin—the feminine, heart centered principle—adding as many water features, weeping trees, and silver trees as I could to change that harsh feeling. So, the people can be much more comfortable and tend to linger now, to hang out more, to be more open, receptive and tuning into the Divine. Now this place encourages people to meditate in a garden, to "pause and smell the roses."

And consequently, we're getting repeat people coming up more often and more people are hearing about it. It's drawing people from town. Occasionally, somebody from town will show up and say, "We heard about this wonderful garden." So, it's fulfilling its plan, it's becoming a place of pilgrimage, because it's a place that you can come and sit and be contemplative.

It's all tied together. This has been an ongoing process, and I've felt privileged to be part of it. I've always seen God in nature. Every place I look out all through this hilltop, I see God. The creations of this garden surely are not coming from me—it's merely coming *through* me. It lets me experience the Divine on a very personal level.

In *The Findhorn Garden* book, one of the nature spirits is saying, "Well, we'll let you humans do that, but not without us creating a bit of mischief along the way." It's true. We've moved all those kinds of wild devas out to Bald Mountain. They just moved out on their own accord. Those types don't like being around people. Those ones out at Bald Mountain just have a different nature. There are hostile devas, and sweet devas, and everything in between. You know, if they don't like you, they can sting! So, I tell people when they walk to Bald Mountain to be sure to stay on the paths. But, up at the Retreat, we have all the domesticated devas. I'm not sure I'm seeing them, or they're telling me, but my attention is being drawn to things that need me. I don't see the devas or the fairies or the little fluttery things. But I know they're there.

I really should have known what to do when the deer started devouring the Meditation Retreat's garden. But working with the nature spirits sensitively just hadn't been our focus at Ananda. At Sirius Community where I had trained—just like they do at Findhorn itself—we meditated all the time, and we talked to the nature spirits. And when the deer would start eating the gardens, we would all meditate and try to feel what to do. One person got something in meditation. It was to try a Bach Flower remedy. Someone else asked, "How are we supposed to give that to the deer?" And someone else said, "Maybe we're supposed to take it ourselves." We did, and the deer stopped eating everything. So, they were responding to our consciousness. Swami talked only a little bit about this. We don't have that focus as much at Ananda.

I personally do a lot more talking *to* the plants and animals than I do hearing back from them. They don't necessarily talk. It comes to me in a different way. It comes more like an *awareness.* Not with a word attached to it—not most of the time. What do they have to talk to *me* about? "I need some water. How 'bout some fertilizer?" But sometimes they *do* tell me something, like at Temenos one time. In the ways I'd been trained from Findhorn, I asked this one set of bushes if it was OK to take them out. But this time it came back, "No, you may not." And I thought, "Oh that's the first 'No' I've ever gotten, that I can remember." And I sat there awhile longer, and then it continued on and said, "But you can *prune* us."

Sometimes we have people up here at the Meditation Retreat who say they can hear the Nature Spirits. They tell me about it, but it doesn't make a lot of difference. I just go, "That's nice." So what? It doesn't change what we must do, and obviously that needed to happen for those people. That's the way they see it and hear it, and I just see it and hear it in my own way.

2020s

FINAL EXAM

It's been a fun life. I have no complaints. It is starting to get a little long. But at least we are getting these stories saved for the future. And look how we all are advancing, and growing, and getting closer to God and Guru. That usually doesn't happen much by age 30, because the early part of our lives is mostly cleaning up karma—and hopefully not making too much more.

It has been an interesting life! When I was telling a Hindu man about my life, and I'd gotten through several of the episodes, he says, "Oh, you have had one of those lives where there's many lives in one life. It's all about fine-tuning." We're doing things to bring up stuff. As soon as you get that thing tuned, you go on to the next adventure. I used to think all the steps were connected. But then it got to the point when they seemed no longer to be connected. Each one is its own lesson. The first ones are to get you going. And then when you finally work up the momentum, watch out! It's like having to ski around the inevitable moguls[9] of life.

Am I a core Ananda person? Well, I've always felt that in a past life I must have been from one of Ananda's neighboring villages. But my own group doesn't have a locus on the planet this time around, so this is the next best place I could be. I do bump into my own people from time to time.

Somehow Devi always understood me, all the way back to when she met me out at Buckhorn Springs. She told me during one of our long talks, "Whenever I talk with you, I have a sense that we're speaking in a foreign language." I tend to think she meant our connection was from a past life. Like when I knew her as my general in a past life.

We obviously go way back together. I think all of us do. Devi accepts me as I am. Durga and Vidura have been the same way with me. I just have a different way—just very individual. They've just accepted that. But I've always been 100% Ananda. Whatever Swami or Ananda would have asked me to do I would have done it.

Whenever I have an illness or a hurt, people ask, "How are you?"

I respond, "I am fine, ... but this body is having a wee bit of trouble." These fragile bodies of ours!

Dalphiniums

Baby Buddha

Cabin with Rhododendrons

Ruth in elder years

Bright Pink Water Lilies

Pond Lilies

It's been hard, because my dear buddy Ruth was away up at Ananda House (our resident facility for elders near Portland, Oregon). It was hard being so far away while her mental abilities were slipping. She remembered less and less about the recent past. Her memory of the distant past is fine. But she and I are so close, I was able to finish her sentences when she could not. I've heard all her stories before, just like she has heard all of mine. So, I could plug in the missing words, and it just flowed without any interruption. We talked for long periods if I added in the little missing pieces. I might be the last person whose name she remembered.

I talked about this with Ruth: "We're in the fourth ashram. Picture yourself like a hot air balloon, and we're all trying to rise up, up to God and to the realm of the Divine. And we can't do that if we don't get rid of these sandbags. The sandbags are all our memories, all our attachments." Then I said to her, "Divine Mother must love you tremendously, look at all the help She's giving you—a lot of lift right now. You don't have to worry about letting those little memories go because they're gone. Mother's helping you release them! There is only one place you have to go now, and that's to God." She understood completely what I was talking about.

When Ruth was still living at Ananda Village, she worked to be in an uplifted state. She kept to herself in her apartment. Even when her car broke down for two months, she didn't go out anywhere unless I picked her up. A few people would stop by occasionally to say hi. All this was while she was living at Villa Luce, one of the big group houses at Ananda Village. But through it all she had a glow about her because she kept herself in a state of uplifted consciousness.

I'm holding Ruthie's ashes after her passing

Ruth always has been ten years older than me, so by 2020 she was over 90 years old. What's taking place for her is appropriate for her age. There are no accidents on this path. Why fight it?

This reminds me about what a friend in Italy told me, who had what I called "His Fighting Family." I was with them for three days. Talk about me needing to cocoon! When they dropped me off at Ananda Assisi, one of them said, "Oh, I'm so happy you were with us! When you are with us, we tend to fight less."

I thought, 'If that was *less* . . .?' I know it's merely their culture. Italians can be emotionally volcanic. Combine that with sibling rivalry—not pretty. These were wonderful people. But it's like they were connected to a sinking rock and wouldn't let go. That's how much of the world can be. It all comes back to this one fact: at Ananda, we have a *wonderful* life. Look at how differently we have been able to experience our lives.

I'm in a moment-to-moment flow these days. I've never been able to write very many letters because I think by the time I mail them, everything's going to be different. That's how rapidly my life changes; I'm a flow. Whenever I'm traveling, like wherever I was in India, I thought, 'OK, if I were stuck here the rest of my life, what would I do?' I'd act appropriately for that setting and figure out how to merge into it—what kind of little stall I would have. It would be only three meters wide, just like everyone else's there. I wouldn't wish to place myself there, but if I found myself having to live under cardboard in the slums of India, I would at least have a very *pretty* cardboard shack.

When I lived in the bottom floor of a brownstone in New York City, I put some planters in the front and had a little garden. The rest of the neighborhood had nothin'. But I started gardening, and suddenly, the whole block started gardening. That's all it takes; a bit of consciousness and it spreads.

Back in the late 80's and early 90's, I remember thinking; 'Enough of this, if I don't know you from before—from past lives—I'm just not as interested in starting new relationships.' Those from past lives are the only connections I'll make, and not even them all the time, because we know an awful lot of people. More and more, I'm realizing how much of the stuff we deal with is not from *this* lifetime but rather is karma from past lives.

I'm not good being around sick people. I just don't know what to do. It was miraculous that I was able to take care of Ananda's first resident Satya during his final year of life. Unreal! I just don't normally do that caretaker thing well. Sometimes, I'd have to take him to the hospital. One time I said to him, "You know, Satya, I've been sitting here with you for six hours. This was a total divine gift. In the past, if I was in here for ten *minutes*, I would be going crazy." But with him I had no problem.

An astrologer warned that there might need to be an attendant for me near the end of life—not for dementia especially—but my mind will be other-worldly, somewhere else. Even now I must pay special attention to things. Things don't come automatically anymore. I can't rely on that as much as I used to. Of course, because of my dyslexia, I've never been able act on autopilot much, anyway. All my life, I've been *forced* to concentrate.

CHARLES' HOPES

For much of my life, it's been hard for me to stay in one place. Amazingly, this time it's been over 20 years here at the Meditation Retreat! I came back to the Retreat in December of 2001. Total of 34 years since first coming to Ananda!

During all those years, I landscaped little bits of *many* of Ananda's colonies around the world. Of course, much that I put in slowly disappears over time. But we at least got the bones of it in place. But there is no retirement on our path. Just like a black hole, it's never finished. Up here at the Retreat I must fight not to get sucked in. I only work half days now. A very important beginner's lesson at Ananda is to learn to say yes, whatever is asked of you. But the more advanced lesson for Ananda people, after you've mastered saying yes, is to learn to say a dharmic no. I often answer to someone who asks me to do something, "I'll meditate on it."

I don't take credit for this garden. I take credit for the labor, for digging the holes. In our society we seldom give much credit to the gardeners. They are among the least paid of the people our society employs. Nevertheless, it's a wonderful position for me to have during this time in my life.

The way I look at it, when Swami was at SRF, they had a balance between both Brahma (the expansive creative) energy and Vishnu (the conserving sustaining) energy. In a complementary whole, each makes up for what the other lacks. But when Swami departed from SRF, it's like he took the expansive creative energy with him. They were left primarily with the conserving sustaining energy. Therefore, they're good at maintaining what they already had.

We at Ananda, on the other hand, have lots of the expansive creative energy, so we're good at new endeavors. Seems to me that SRF suffers because they are not great at being expansive, and we at Ananda suffer because we're not great at maintaining things. What each of our organizations need to do is to grow that other half.

How many times has this Retreat been re-invented? If we were better at maintaining things, we wouldn't need all these major re-dos. At present, because of Vidura and Durga's leadership, we are in real good shape up here at the Retreat. Crystal Hermitage has wonderful landscaping, and Villa Luce—what we used to call Sundance—has some landscaping. There's a modicum of it. Those are just a few places. But most of our houses at Ananda Village have none. It wouldn't take much. Six bushes would often be enough. You wouldn't want it to look like you were in a suburb, with green lawns and things, but at least enough to break the starkness. Too often landscaping gets put into place, but then is allowed to dissipate. I look forward to the day when staffing to maintain its landscaping raises to a higher priority for Ananda.

As Nischala put it, "Like everything at Ananda, you must put focus into it, and will power. A lot of people love this garden here at the Retreat. It's like a sanctuary. It's taken a lot of *tapasya* from a lot of people to create it. Let's hope we keep it up so even more of us can enjoy it in the future."

THE GARDEN'S FUTURE

Satya, that old friend of mine, was up here at the Meditation Retreat in the very beginning with Swami. In Ananda's earliest years, Satya actually used to run the Retreat himself. He lived much of his adult life right here on the Retreat property. Nischala, who ran the college here, told this story about him: "Satya came up to me, after we'd done a lot of the garden, and said excitedly, 'Nischala, Nischala'—which in itself was unusual because he hardly ever spoke— 'I had this dream many years ago: the whole Meditation Retreat was a garden, and these white-robed people were here' (like for our graduations, or for kriya initiations.) Now this dream was something like fifty years ago—very early on in the late 60's. But Satya had been seeing the future of what was going to come about. From the very beginning there has been a plan for this Retreat in the ethers."

Actually, I try not to have expectations for the garden's future. The garden is what it is. All that I foresee is that it's a place to be calm and meditate and to connect with the Divine. If the garden does that, my dreams are fulfilled.

When the Ananda College moved away from here to Laurelwood, the garden at the Meditation Retreat went into a bit of a demise, largely because for a while it was just *me* doing the work. One real good helper who came after the college departed was Ann, the one who did the long "Camino" walk in Spain. She both knew about gardening *and* was intuitive. Thank God, she was here for over a year.

John Carlsen was another big help lately because he, too, was intuitive. He was a blessing. He knew nothing about plants when he got here, so I had him read *The Findhorn Garden* book. Very soon he was figuring things out on this own. John has intuition—a big heart, and a lot of compassion—and he knew how to listen.

When we were getting ready for the 50th Anniversary of Ananda celebration, the front of our temple area here at the Meditation Retreat was a disaster. Stuff had died. I always knew we needed to re-landscape that, but there's never enough time. But I had John, and I was in town, and I saw one plant. It was a very expensive plant, but it would anchor the whole project. Once I had the plant that would ground the project, the rest just fell into place. I didn't even have to think. I'd walk through, and I'd just say, "This one, this one, this one, and this one." I go into an altered state. And I get them all home, but I don't know what I'm going to do with them. Yet, with John's help, they all came together.

As Nischala put it, "I hope someday we'll have somebody who will take responsibility for the garden, add to it, and ensure it won't just dry up."

I don't actively recruit people to work here, but I sure appreciate when a good one shows up.

Workers don't usually stay here very long. They don't realize it but it's too intense. You really can't stay up here if you don't learn how to stay open all the time. It'll just beat you to a pulp. You just have to say, "OK." The place is helping you to correct things in yourself. It's not causing any big problems, unless you try to block that energy. Most people do just that, because that much energy coming at you is uncomfortable. It's a *tapasya* (self-discipline for purification). It brings up stuff people don't want to know.

Not long ago, I told Master, "I'm doing what I can do. If you need it to look better, it's up to you." I really mean that. Sometimes yes, I get frustrated, because I don't like shabby things. But then I remind myself, "You can only fix as much as you can do."

To see any of these plants suffer, it hurts me. It's like they're my children. It's real hard for me to stand back and allow the garden to do what it's going to do. It's like standing back and allowing your children to make mistakes. I try to calm my fears by thinking, 'They're gonna do what they're gonna do!' I try to use Swami as my example. I got here in 1993—December '92, actually. I watched Swami pull back his active engagement from Ananda. I just noticed as time went on that he was less and less hands-on. And there were some obvious mistakes being made that only he could have corrected. I knew he knew it. But in order for others to learn, he did *nothing* about it. Otherwise, his followers wouldn't get the strength and the discrimination they would need later on, and there are only so many hours in the day.

Currently, I'm deliberately very hard on these plants. I am not pampering them. I am preparing them for hard times. It's going to happen. When I'm not in the Retreat Garden every morning to be sure those plants are doing fine, they suffer. Look at what's happened to the Lahiri Shrine at the Expanding Light over the years. It nestles the Shrine in there. That hedge is doing exactly what it was supposed to do—to protect the shrine from distracting noises on the path above it. What's around Lahiri Shrine now is OK—Biraj and I gave it good bones. But some of the beauty that was once there is gone. It takes intense attention to keep a garden in its prime. We still create beauty up here at the Meditation Retreat Garden. Even though it will be harder when I'm gone, there will still be a good foundation on which to build the future garden.

Some people are worried about what's going to happen. People have to stop over-worrying. This is not *our* concern. We just need to do what's in front of us, then wait and see. Master must send someone to take this on. But let's see what He and Mother have in mind. Now, that does not excuse us from doing our part.

It's always good to remember the wisdom from one of my favorite movies, *The Best Exotic Marigold Hotel*: "Everything turns out fine in the *end*. So, if it's not fine yet, it must not be the end!"

THE GURU'S POWER

Ever since coming back in 2018 from Ananda's center at Laurelwood (outside Portland, Oregon,) where I had been working on the placement for Master's statue, I'm much more at ease up here at the Retreat. Before Laurelwood, I was really looking to get out of here. I get wound up like that sometimes. I'm just not a sedentary person. But what happened up at Laurelwood got my attention.

Byasa Steinmetz, and even more so his wife Janakadevi, had been trying to get me up there the previous three years. What finally got me up there was my good buddy Ruth having to move up to Ananda House (the elders' residence) at Laurelwood. I took her up there, and once I'd done that I realized, "Yes, I'm supposed to do this statue project." So, we had gone through everything, gotten the hill ready, and gotten the statue up, and all of that. Jyotish and Devi were doing the dedication weekend, and as part of it, they led the ceremony down in the big hall on campus to declare the statue a living murti.

Because I was part of this program, I had to sit up in the front row. And you know how much I do not like being in the limelight! I don't much like the attention I get. It's more than enough that I lead garden tours a few times a month. But I became sort of a mega-star up at Laurelwood. I got more fame there than I'm comfortable with. I prefer to be more of a stage manager behind the scenes than the star performer out on the stage.

The photo of Master that came alive

During the Saturday that weekend, I had to give a small five-minute talk. I was already blissful in response to that. Then that Sunday, during Sunday Service, all I can say is the light changed in that auditorium, at least for me. Things got less defined. It was a bit like looking through rippling water, except for that beautiful picture of Yogananda that I always have thought was too pretty.

That picture came alive. Yogananda was present. I can't explain much about it, except that it was one of the most wonderful experiences I have ever known. Again, it took me right into total bliss. And that's when I got an inner message that said: "It's OK to continue to play for now. But there is a task coming." It was like that time up in Ashland, when I heard, "Yes, you can get another job, but it has to be just like this one." I knew then that any new one wasn't going to be any easier.

"There is a task coming" was followed immediately by, "I thought I was *done* with tasks!" The word 'task' didn't sound like it was going to be a light thing. I felt a heaviness to the word. This intuition sounded almost exactly like the one Biraj got one time. How did that one go? "Don't worry too much about things right now, but I'm getting you ready for the next task. It's going to be a doozy!" You sort of want to shake in your boots with that kind of guidance. But I bet 'the task' will end up being good. It will keep me going, and motivated. It seems not yet to be my time to slow down.

Do I have a choice about taking on this next task? No, it didn't sound like it. Seemed like I got 'volunteered!' The thought came, 'Well, just forget about it, and enjoy yourself for *now.*' So, I continue to play.

That whole weekend up at Laurelwood, Yogananda was present. And in that statue, he was most definitely present to me. It perfectly fulfilled the definition of a murti, of embodying the Spirit of Divinity.

The moment I think about certain things, I go into that near-teary bliss. That time when Yogananda's photo came alive to me was one of those moments. Devi spotted me having that experience. At some point, I looked up at her, and she was intently staring right into me. I think she knew something magical had happened. Several times during that Sunday Service, I felt she was tuning in to what was going on with me. We have a very close connection. Sometimes, it even seems like she's remembering another life where we were close. When she mentioned me in her talk over that weekend for Yogananda Garden, it gave me a thrill. She's my queen.

Those events up in Laurelwood that weekend switched my whole attitude. Now I'm fine doing the simple maintenance, doing whatever I can do. It said, 'Enjoy yourself for a while.' The maintenance here is mindless work. The only thing that's hard is not *reacting* to it. When I see things going wrong, I have to question if it's supposed to happen: Can I fix it? *Should* I fix it? Once you start realizing that every action has all these repercussions, it's like Chaos Theory's metaphor of the butterfly flapping its wings in Japan resulting in a hurricane hitting the Caribbean. Everything that we do puts a vibration out into the world. I think as we grow in this path, we become more and more aware of that.

I don't sit very often. I'm usually moving around doing things. That's how I relax. When I come home after work, I'll putter on my deck, potting some plants, or vacuum. I'm not a sedentary kind of person. I sit later in the evening. I'll watch a TV program or a movie. Before that, though, I want to keep moving. I suspect the garden is thankful for my OCD. I'm truly peripatetic. But you know, this garden at its current size is about all that one person can handle. In fact, about one quarter is as much as I can watch closely. The rest I've had to let go. It's going to do what it's going to do.

A basic operating principle in my life is—I know from observing myself—that I like to create beauty. I'm just a magnet for pretty things. I like to put things in balance. I have kind of a *feng shui* eye. What I see are a lot of things that are out of place. Then either I put them in place, or I choose to ignore them. It's been a blessing to be able to learn what to ignore, and what not to ignore. I've had to learn more every day to get comfortable with ignoring some things even though they're in the wrong place. That makes it easier on me, but that achievement has only come recently.

It doesn't mean that I don't get a little sad at times. Sad not so much that it isn't working out like I hoped, but more because the plant is suffering a bit: I planted you there, and now you're having trouble, it's empathy. I'll be walking down the path, and I'm seeing everything. 'Oh, no! Water problem here, bug problem over there.' *I'm* not exactly sure whether I'm seeing it, or that *they're* telling me, but my attention is being drawn there.

I've had a blessed life. I must be careful not to abuse that. I have no idea why everyone was so protective when I was in my teens and twenties. Why did Peter Shane, the big burly football lineman, protect me in high school?

Charles in his vest

There's just something in me that attracts that. So you know, I have to be careful, because I could get away with murder. It's like when someone has charisma, it's not their fault. I've had to resist the thought that others think I should be a leader. Early on in this spiritual journey, I had an awareness that I was *not* to be a minister, and not to develop a following or a congregation. I've known about that since the 1980's. Here at Ananda, they wanted me to be a minister, but I said, "No, I can't." They told me that *that* attitude makes the best kind of minister. I still had to say no. I'm very careful about that. I can do one-on-one. But a public ministry is not what this lifetime is about for me. My ministering takes a different form; it's private, it's not flashy. And yes, I guess I do have a following of sorts, whether I want it or not. But most of the time, I *don't* want it. My initial reaction is more often, "Could you just leave me alone and let me water."

I often say things to people that sort of stops them in their tracks—like it's the answer they're looking for. I was chatting with our late friend Jagadish Franklin and his wife Shanta one day, and Shanta says, "God just spoke through you." It just happens. I stay open and somehow access wisdom that not everyone is listening to. I think that's one of the reasons I talk non-stop, because I never know when it will come out. Here at the Retreat, I'll pass someone on the paths, and I'll just be chatting about something, and *boom!* They get just what they needed. It's the same thing that allows me to know where to put this plant. I just *know* things. Something just pops in. I have no idea about it before I say it. It just comes.

Of course, sometimes it gets perceived differently. I don't filter what comes out of my mouth. I have that ability to see inside people, and many of them aren't really wanting to know that much about themselves.

I kept asking on my car trip across the Southwest, and finally discovered my totem was an owl. One time I came across a dead owl. I took its wing tips and kept them for a long time. I seem to fit the Native American description of owl energy. Then one time at an apartment building in New York City I was at a Native American gathering. Out in the hall I asked one of the people about it, saying "I've been told I have owl energy."

Instantly they said, "Shhhhhh. The whole room will empty out!" People are afraid of owl energy because they say owl people can see in the dark.

It's an odd responsibility, knowing things that others don't seem to. The odd things I do, don't come from rational thinking at all, it's all intuition.

It's not about "the devil made me do it." Rather it's "Mother made me do it!" The Divine Mother.

Oh, on the other hand .... I suppose occasionally it *is* about the other one.

AFTERWORD

By Biraj Palmer

So, on one level, this book is merely a collection of stories—stories with which Charles Evans regaled me over the 30 years I've known him.

But what does it all mean?

Charles has humbly given his time and talent to transform a virtual desert into a paradise. He's done it with quiet, understated humor. And perhaps with a wee bit of pixie dust ... because the results seem a bit like a miracle.

What is it that makes what Charles has accomplished so special? I believe it's primarily his faith in, and reliance on, his inner intuition—the wisdom that comes from what he fondly refers to as "Mother." All the most dramatic moments in his storied life—and there have been many—seem to have come by his hearing, and listening to, guidance from this inner source.

I once told Charles that the main motivation for my compiling this book was to show "how the Divine has made use of a soul who was willing to listen." And Charles responded enthusiastically, "That's my whole mission with the garden tours and everything I do here. If *I* can do it, *you* can do it, too! It's all about tuning it."

And so it is.

Charles lives totally in the present moment. You might have noticed in the stories he tells, he rarely uses anything other than the present tense.

Charles spends time neither in regrets of the past, nor in worries about the future, but in the present moment. He is always listening for whatever "Mother" wants him to do. Not that he always surrenders right away. In much the same way that Ananda's guru, Paramhansa Yogananda, did,

Charles often argues with Divine Mother, halfway hoping She might give him an assignment more to his liking. But in the end, he usually surrenders to Her will.

What I recall most, as I think back over the times I've spent with Charles and listened to his stories, is a delightful twinkle in his eye. So much of what he says sounds like he's half-joking. Charles finds delight in all the events of his life — perhaps even more so in the challenging ones.

The last time I visited Charles, I found him in a corner of his garden seldom seen by the casual visitor. He calls this place, "the orphanage"—a private sanctuary for plants who don't yet have a home, or who had struggled a bit where they were. I found Charles clad in his trademark, faded baseball cap, ministering to his orphans. Charles, garden hose in hand, was giving life-sustaining water to his beloved plants. With that famous twinkle in his eye, Charles said, "Here in my orphanage, I can keep a closer eye on 'em."

Charles' love for his plant friends gave birth to the Ananda Meditation Retreat Garden. That love is tangible, and the plants feel it. They respond to that love.

Whenever you or I take the time to stroll, or quietly sit, amidst this amazing garden, we too can feel something special, something ethereal ...

The plants are loving us back.

ENDNOTES

1 Chutzpah – A Yiddish word that means extreme self-confidence or bravery that borders on rudeness.

2 Sattwa is a calming force characterized by qualities of positivity, balance, and serenity. Sattwic is used often by Ananda people referring to that calming, centering quality in people, places and foods.

3 Akashic records are an archive, a dimension of consciousness, that tells the story of your soul's journey through space and time—past, present and future—as a human being.

4 Dyslexia is a learning disability that affects reading or writing.

5 Antipathy is a noun that means a strong feeling of dislike or aversion.

6 Bharat Cornell is an Ananda Minister, a teacher of Kriya Yoga and the founder and president of Sharing Nature Worldwide, one of the planet's most popular and influential environmental education programs.

7 SRF - Self Realization Fellowship, Paramhansa Yogananda's original organization in America, in which Swami Kriyananda served from 1948-1961

8 Serviceful-a word coined at Ananda to refer to someone who often engages in voluntary service.

9 Mogul bumps on snowy hillsides thrown up by the sharp turnings of previous skiers

Photo Attributions

Photos by Barbara Bingham

Photos by Kent Williams

Photos by Charles Evans

Photos by Biraj Palmer

Charles M. Evans

Charles Evans has followed an extraordinary path in life. Now Now he is locally famous as a somewhat eccentric gardener at one of the best-established spiritual retreats in Northern California.

He prepared himself for his eventual career with a range of often comic adventures including: high school teacher, art gallery owner, retail store designer, head chef, carpenter, high-rise building superintendent, health food clerk, vegetable salesman, and even as a cowboy.

The common thread running through all these experiences has been that Charles listens for inner guidance. He claims that his ability to rise to the top in all these endeavors has been due merely to the fact that he is willing to listen—and to follow—the intuition that makes Itself known to him. Guided by this inner practice, starting in 2001 Charles took a virtual desert and transformed it into a lush oasis. He still lives, gardens, and give tours at the Ananda Meditation Retreat outside Nevada City, California.

Biraj Wayne Palmer

Biraj Palmer, after a decade-long career in Montessori education, moved in 1984 to Ananda Village, an intentional spiritual community of meditators. Throughout the 90's, Biraj led weekend programs for the public at Ananda's Expanding Light Retreat near Nevada City, California. Biraj and his wife Lahari were founding members of Ananda's ministry in India, and recently worked for most of a year successfully helping Narayani and Shurjo Jha strengthen the Ananda community in Mumbai, India. Both Lahari and Biraj adore singing and kirtan chanting, while also being known for their counseling and listening skills.

As a surprise even to themselves, the two of them spent three growing seasons launching Ananda Palo Alto's now-flourishing farm along California's coast at Half Moon Bay. Biraj's previous book was *Heart Calls, Soul Answers: Communicating with Your Higher Self.*

Publisher
Robin Heerens Lysne

Robin Heerens Lysne, M.A., M.F.A., Ph.D, is the author of twelve books, an artist and energy medicine practitioner, medium and psychic. Currently she launched her two new books, *Two Worlds One Light, A Memoir of a Medium, The Mother of Us All: Divine Mother Speaks: A Way Forward. The Mother of Us All* book, just got an International Impact Book Award in January of 2025. She publishes other books by authors in poetry, fiction and non-fiction.

Her first two books were published by Conari Press. Her poems have been published in: North American Review, Catamaran, Porcupine Literary Arts Magazine, Monterey Bay Poetry Review, Rattle, Phren-z online Magazine, Porter Gulch Review, Samizdat, Awakening Consciousness Magazine, and others.

On her days not writing, she paints, offers clients energy medicine, psychic readings, akashic record readings, and mediumistic readings. She mentors others who are coming into their abilities. She also teaches Energy Medicine and Intuition, and Guides and Spirit Guides workshops.

She is a part of Ananda Monterey Bay, and visits the Ananda Village and The Ananda Retreat Center regularly since 2014. Her websites are: www.thecenterforthesoul.com, www.robinlysne.com and www.bluebonebooks.com.

Blue Bone Books
Santa Cruz, CA

Blue Bone Books Publications by Robin H. Lysne:

The Mother of Us All: Divine Mother Speaks - A Way Forward, 2024
Winner of the International Impact Book Award, 2025
Two Worlds One Light, A Memoir of a Medium, 2024

The Legendary Ancestral Women's Series:

Narrative Non-Fiction
Kisti's Royal Garden, 2023

Novels
The Legend of Randine: Entering the Sisterhood, 2021
The Legend of Randine: The Laerdal Letters, 2022

Poetry
Mosaic: New and Collected Poems, 2017
Poems for the Lost Deer, 2014

Non-Fiction
Ceremonies from the Heart, for Children, Adults and the Earth, 2018
Heart Path, Learning to Love Yourself and Listening to Your Guides, 2006
Heart Path Handbook, for Therapists and Healers, 2014
all published by Blue Bone Books, Santa Cruz, CA
Sacred Living, 365 Meditations and Celebrations, 2000
Dancing Up the Moon, A Woman's Guide to Creating
Traditions that Bring Sacredness to Daily Life, 1995
(both published by Conari Press) and *Luminaria*
a new poetry book ready for publication

BBB Books Published from Other Authors:

Author: Barbara Thomas

Infused with the Muse,
Poetry, Prose and Rambling
Thoughts. poetry, prose, 2021
Emerald Street Poets, Uneasthed, poetry, 2020

Author: Biraj Wayne Palmer

Heart Calls, Soul Answers, non-fiction prose, 2019

Stuart Presley, Visible Light, poetry, 2018
Janet Trenchard, Infared, poetry, 2016

Author: Amita

You Long For Me, A devotional Offering to the
Divine Presence in Each of Us, non-fiction prose, 2014
Margaret Bond Smith, Summer Street, Family Stories, 2008